Slaves
To BISHOPS
An American Story

WHAT READERS SAY

Slaves to Bishops provides a fresh and readable account of the story of African-American Methodism with some special emphasis on the Delmarva Peninsula. Using new research the book demonstrates that, far from being a minor part of the Methodist story, African Americans were a central to the Methodist Movement in America, starting with George Whitefield's preaching in Lewes, Delaware, in 1739. The book brings the history down to the present day including not only Black participation in The United Methodist Church but also the independent African Methodist denominations.

Philip Lawton, Ph.D.
Conference Historian
The Peninsula-Delaware Conference The United Methodist Church

At last, an inclusive look at the beginnings of American Methodism on the Delmarva Peninsula. Focusing a powerful lens, *Slaves to Bishop*s spotlights the under-recognized work of African Americans in the early Methodist Church. This easy to understand accounting makes plain the structure and culture of the nascent church. All readers of Methodist history will appreciate the concise descriptions of how the church functioned back in the day.

Anthony B. Johnson
Local Delaware Historian
Dale UMC, Middletown, Delaware and Singing Praying Bands of Maryland and Delaware.

Slaves To Bishops

An American Story

By Gary L. Moore

1740 Publishers
Easton, MD

Slaves To Bishops: An American Story
Moore, Gary L.
You may contact the author at: slaves2bishops@gmail.com

ISBN
Paperback: 979-8-9944145-0-7

Published 2025 by 1740 Publishers
Easton, Maryland

Library of Congress Control Number: 2025927729

Edited and Proofread by WriteBooksRight

Book cover and interior layout design
By Eddie Egesi, Apricot Press (An imprint of Apricot Branding)

All royalties from the purchase of this book will be donated toward the support of African-American Methodism at Barratt's Chapel and Museum:
6362 Bay Road
Frederica, Delaware 19946

(www.barrattschapel.org)

To My Wife,
Jeanne Ellen Morgan Moore

&

My First Counseling Elder and
Lover of the Delaware Conference,
The Rev. Dr. W. Hayward Greene

A Kongo Crucifix (Nkangi Kiditu)

(Brooklyn Museum) Early 17th Century

Used with permission

TABLE OF CONTENTS

INTRODUCTION

A Black Son Is Named "Asberry"

Francis Asbury, being the only missionary to remain in America during the American Revolution, had become the default leader of American Methodists. For three successive days over Christmas 1784, the founders of the Methodist Episcopal Church met in Baltimore and ordained him deacon, elder, and consecrated him bishop. This solidified his ascendency as the undisputed leader of American Methodists. By the time of his death in 1816, more Americans had seen him than any other person in America. This was made possible by his annual practice of traveling the length of the East Coast, starting in South Carolina. It is estimated he traveled 130,000 miles mostly on horseback and sought housing for the night from ordinary people. Not only did they see him, they got to know him personally. A century after his death, an equestrian statue of the Bishop was designed by Henry Augustus Lukeman and erected in Washington, D.C. at 16th and Mount Pleasant Street, Northeast. Just eight years after becoming bishop, a free Talbot County, Maryland African man in 1792 named his enslaved newborn son, Asberry[1] (Asbury was pronounced as-BERRY). The moniker signified the importance—even the celebrity of American Methodism's most famous leader. Early on and for a long time after him, African Americans named their churches and sons after him.

The earliest known reference to naming is 1790. The spellings vary between the phonetic 'Asberry' and the formal 'Asbury.' Occasionally, parents used his full name, 'Francis Asbury.' Here are examples of the practice:

- Thomas Asberry Asbury, Sr, was born in 1752 in Fauquier County, Virginia. He named his son after him; Thomas Asberry Asbury, Jr, who was born in 1790 in Harrison County, West Virginia. Both were born into slavery. Since the Bishop did not arrive in America until 1771, could their naming have taken place upon their freedom or on their becoming Methodists? It looks like the father took his name as an adult.

- Asberry Chambers was born in 1792 in Frederick County, Maryland, as a free man.

- Asbury Baynardo was born free in 1826 in Caroline County, Maryland.

- Francis Asberry Dorsey was born into slavery in 1832 in Frederick, Maryland.

---

1   *Talbot County Court (Land Records)* 1800-1802, MSA C1880-39, James Earle, Jr. to negro Richard Bowlin, 1802, p. 435. He paid 30 pounds to gain his seven-year-old son's freedom. Two years later, he raised 18 pounds 15 shillings to gain the freedom of his daughter, Maria.

- 1832 Maryland Census of Free Blacks for Queen Anne's County, Maryland, list eleven children ages 8 months to 18 years old named Asbury or Asberry.
- Asberry Johnson was born free in Queen Anne's County, Maryland, in 1836.
- Asbury Ridout was elected an Exhorter in Talbot County in 1856.
- In Trappe, Maryland, on August 6, 1850, the Willis Diary records – 'had his negro Asbury…'
- Asbury Grinnage, a local preacher, was ordained a deacon in the Delaware Conference in July 1865.
- In Kent County, Maryland, a church trustee had the name Asbury in 2012.

Is there any higher esteem for a white bishop than to have African Methodists name their sons after Francis Asbury? What was it about him and American Methodism that fostered such regard?

The purpose of this work is to show that African Americans were not "Johnny-come-latelies" to the story of American Methodism. From its earliest days, Methodism was Black and white; African Americans were always Methodists.

Wade Crawford Barclay observed that in 1787: "It is evident, with more than six thousand Negroes enrolled as Church members within the first three years of the Church's life, that at least some of the Circuit Riders and Local Preachers were giving more than casual attention to ministry to the slaves."[2]

The trauma of the Civil War has shattered how we understand the origins of African-American Methodism. This work is an attempt to understand the movement that created African-American Methodism from its beginnings to the shattering brought on by the Civil War.

A second purpose is to clarify what scholars often seem to overlook or misunderstand: Methodism is a connectional, not a congregational, system. A simple way to illustrate 'a connectional system' is as a Rubik's Cube. All the pieces are tied together and remain together, even when one part is moved, it maintains its shape. This is addressed in the chapter 'How Methodism Functioned.' My approach is to weave a thread of history from the Colonial Period to the Civil War using primary sources. As with all historical writing, the lack of extant documents has kept us from a better understanding of the early attraction Methodism had for African Americans. The most important documents are the Quarterly Conference Minutes. While they were carefully recorded, they have not been well preserved. Fortunately for me, the Talbot Quarterly Conference records are complete from 1805 to the Civil War.

2　Wade Crawford Barclay, *History of Methodist Missions: Early American Methodism 1769-1844* Vol. I (Board of Missions and Church Extension of The Methodist Church, 1949), page 268.

Another struggle is the human blindness people have toward people different from themselves. In the sources, African Americans were always present but seldom 'seen' by the writers. The times when they are 'seen' by the writer gives us a glimpse into their desire to be Christian and Methodist.

This writer recognizes that African-American Methodism existed in a place where slavery was the law of the land. There are many accounts of the unjust way people were treated and the extreme limitations on their personal agency. The focus here is on the Methodist Episcopal Church and the unique form of Christianity, African or Black Methodism, that was developed within it by a people whose lives were extremely constricted by the larger society.

African American Methodist Historical Tree

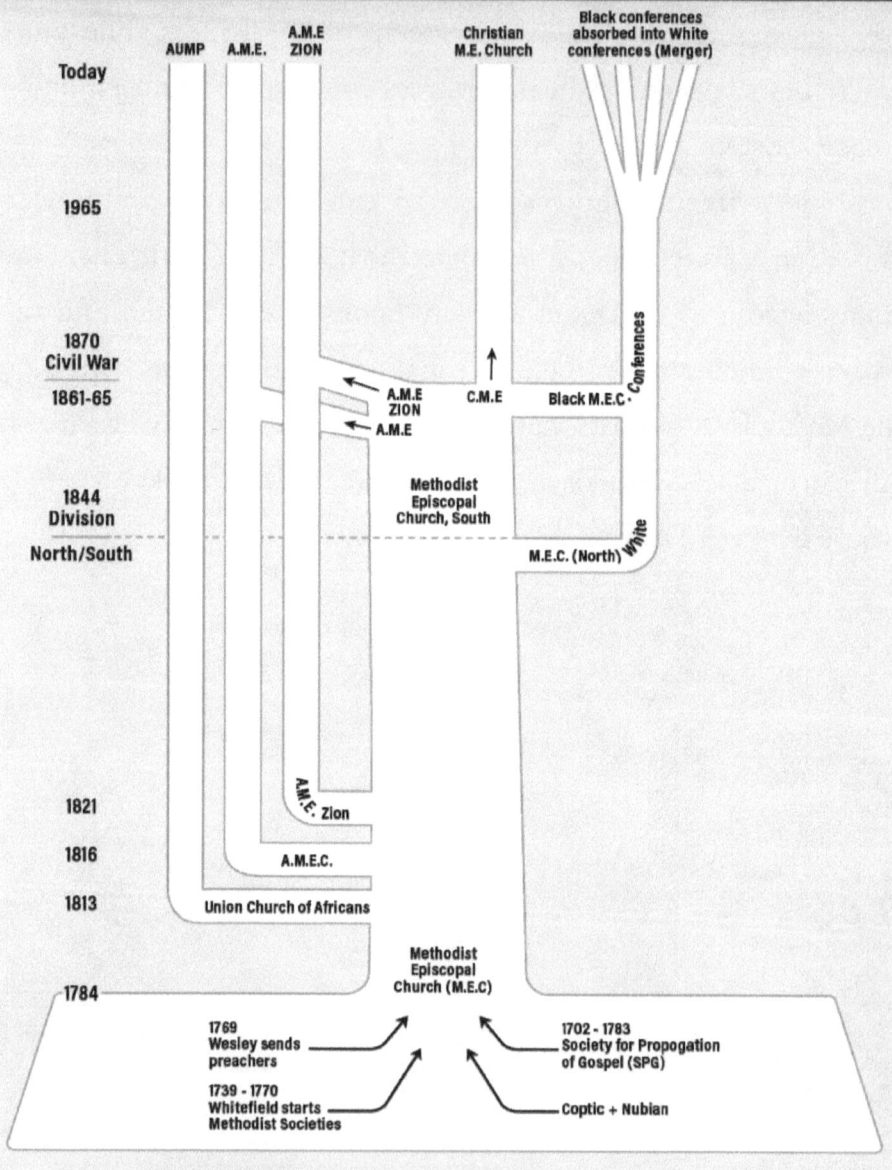

LEGEND   AMEC: African Methodist Episcopal Church   CMEC: Christian Methodist Episcopal Church
               AME Zion: African Methodist Episcopal Zion Church   AUMP: Spencer Churches

CHAPTER 1

African Christianity

The cover of this book shows an early seventeenth-century brass crucifix illustrated with traditional African images and craftsmanship.[3] It illustrates that Christianity existed in Africa before it came to America. The history of European Christianity is well known; the early African-Christian history is unknown to us. Before telling the American story, a brief review is required of the highlights of African Christianity before Africans became enslaved and sent to the Americas.

The story begins with an African, John Mark, an associate of Peter, and the writer of the Gospel of Mark. His mother lived in the center of the early Christian movement. Born in Africa, she moved to Jerusalem and provided a safe place for Jesus' disciples (Acts 12). She may have hosted the Upper Room Passover for Jesus.[4] Her son, Mark, returned to Africa as its first bishop and was martyred on a street

3   Kongo Crucifx (Nkangi Kiditu), early 17th Century, Brooklyn Art Museum. Used with permission.

4   Thomas Oden, *The African Memory of Mark*, (Downers Grove: InterVarsity Press), page 91. As understood by Sawirus and Shenouda.

in Alexandria. All subsequent African bishops have descended from him in apostolic succession, by which all clergy can trace the sequence of their ordination from bishop to bishop back to the first apostles. The New Testament book of Acts 9 records the meeting of Phillip and the Ethiopian eunuch, who had charge of the Ethiopian queen's treasury. Phillip found him reading from the prophet Isaiah. He was knowledgeable about Judaism and Jewish scriptures. Upon explanation of the Isaiah text, he asked to be baptized by Phillip. This encounter shows the early exposure of Africans to Christianity. We want to ask: Could he have become an early Christian missionary to Ethiopia after he returned home?

Over time, the belief in the Gospel moved up the Nile River and across Ethiopia to Africa's west coast. By the sixth century, Nubian Christians had built a monastery, which had a nativity scene on a wall showing the holy family and sub-Saharan Africans worshiping Christ.[5]

In 1443, Ethiopian church leaders showed up at the Council of Florence, forty-one years after an unsuccessful attempt to influence Rome[6] to help them. Their presence awakened Portuguese interest in Ethiopia and Africa in general.

From 1672 to 1700, thirty-seven Capuchin missionaries recorded 341,000 baptisms in the Kingdom of Kongo. Lamin Sanneh estimated that 40 percent of the total number of transatlantic enslaved

---

5   Dr. Vince Bantu, Bisrat, YouTube, 2022.

6   Ricard Gray, edited by Lamin Sanneh, *Christianity, the Papacy, and Missionary in Africa* (Orbis Books: Maryknoll, NY, 2012), page 5.

people came from the Kongo—Angola area.[7] The mini-series *Roots* could have begun with the Christian baptism of Kunta Kinte by an African Catholic priest, instead of a Muslim ritual.

On the east coast of Africa, Mombasa was the site where seventy-two Christian African men and women chose death rather than conversion to Islam. Another four hundred defiant Christian Africans were taken as slaves to Arabia in exchange for ammunition.

Farther down the coast was Mozambique, which had by 1586 an estimated membership of 2,000 Christians.[8] Robert Gray shared an early 18th-century story of a few slaves on a ship near Tripoli. When the bells were rung for Christian worship, these slaves, originally from northern Nigeria and Christian, went with other Christians to the service.[9]

We have no way of understanding how many slaves were Christians in Africa before their enslavement. What we do know is that Christianity was a 'Black man's' story before it was a 'white Protestant' story.

---

7   Ibid, pages 16-17.
8   Ibid, page 32.
9   Robert Gray, *Journal of African History* (1967), (Cambridge University), pages 383-393

*After a passage of nine weeks from London, on the
20th of October [1769] we made land, and on the 21st,
landed at Gloucester Point [New Jersey], six miles
below Philadelphia. When we got on shore, we joined
in a Doxology and gave praise to God for our deliverance
and all the mercies bestowed upon [us] during the
passage.*

Journal of Joseph Pilmore, pages 19-20.

CHAPTER 2

Asbury Discovers African-American Methodism

Joseph Pilmore, the first missionary to America sent by John Wesley, arrived in New Jersey on October 22, 1769. Two years later, in Philadelphia, he wrote in his Journal on November 10, 1771:

> After morning preaching, a person put a Letter into my hands from a poor Negro slave, part of which ran thus—

> Dear Sir, These are to acquaint you that my bondage is such that I cannot possible attend with the rest of the Class to receive my Ticket; therefore beg you will send it. I wanted much to come to the Church at the Watch-Night but could not get leave; but, I bless God that night, I was greatly favored with the spirit of prayer, and enjoyed much of his divine presence. I find the enemy of my soul continually striving to throw me off the foundation, but I have that within me which bids defiance of his delusive snares. I beg an interest in your prayers that I may be enabled to bear up under all my difficulties with patient resignation to the will of God.[10]

---

10   Joseph Pilmore, *Journal*, November 3-10, 1771. [The week of Monday, November 6, 1769 he writes on page 26 '...and many of the poor Africans are obedient to the faith'.]

This Methodist slave wanted to attend the Watch Night service, but his work for his owner kept him on the job. That Watch-Night Service was held on November 3, one week after Francis Asbury had arrived in Philadelphia. Had the slave been able to attend, he would have met Asbury. To put it another way: There were active Black Methodist slaves in America before Asbury!

Asbury had just arrived from England. In England, he would have met very few African slaves and no African English Methodists. Imagine for a moment Asbury's first experience of America: he sees freed Africans along with slaves walking the streets, working in shops as craftsmen, and in homes as domestic servants. Africans were everywhere. After only seven days, he attends a Watch-Night service where there are Africans fully participating as Methodists in the service.[11] He could easily see the glow of the Spirit expressed in their voices and on their faces. A Watch-Night service was only for those invited by Wesley's appointed leader, and a ticket was required for admittance. This is why the slave so earnestly wanted his ticket.

In these seven days, Asbury was immersed in a world opposite to what he had known in England. Its impact would cause him to dedicate the rest of his life to America and vigorously continue the development of African-American Methodism. He had seen his parents for the last time. His work among American Africans was just beginning.

---

11   Elmer T. Clark, editor, *The Journal and Letters of FRANCIS ASBURY In Three Volumes. Volume 1: The Journal,* (Abingdon Press: Nashville, 1958), p. 7. Hereafter: *Asbury, Journal.*

CHAPTER 3

Africans Find Anglican Christianity Through Baptism

The early development of African-American Methodism goes back seventy years before Asbury arrived in Philadelphia. The Church of England sought to address the spiritual and moral needs of Colonial America. It is here that Africans found Anglican Christianity, often in the form of the Society for the Propagation of the Gospel in Foreign Parts (SPG).

The SPG was formed by Dr. Thomas Bray in response to his time in Maryland as a Commissary for the King. The lack of morals and spirituality in the colonies struck his soul deeply. He returned to England to receive approval from the Bishop of London, who was responsible for the spiritual oversight of all the British colonies worldwide, to start the SPG. Although it had its own organization, it served under the authority of the Bishop of London and all the missionary clergy were Church of England ministers.

Church of England clergy and the operations of the church were part of the Royal Crown's colonies. The SPG sought to provide clergy for those colonies that could not support a pastor. Since Virginia and Maryland were financially viable to support their own clergy and parishes, the work of the SPG was in the other eleven colonies.

The parish system of the Church of England was set up for Anglican clergy to serve all people within the parish and not just Anglicans. Within the work of the parish, the SPG was given the special mission to evangelize African slaves and Native Americans. The Bishop of London, Edmund Gibson, wrote a May 19, 1727, letter to all English slaveholders in America, which was to be delivered personally by the clergy appointed to that area:

> … [L]et me beseech you to consider them, not barely as enslaved people, and upon the same level with laboring beasts, but as Men— enslaved people and Women—enslaved people, who have the same fame and faculties with yourselves and have souls capable of being eternally happy, and reason and understanding to receive instruction in order to it. …

> Let them see, in you and your families, examples of sobriety, temperance and chastity, and all the other virtues and graces of the Christian life. Let them observe how strictly you oblige yourselves, and all that belong to you, to abstain from cursing and swearing, and to keep the Lord's Day holy, and to attend the public worship of God, and the Ordinances which Christ has appointed in his Gospel. Make them sensible, by the general tenor of your behavior and conversation, that your inward temper and disposition is such

as the Gospel requires, that is to say, mild, gentle, and merciful; and that as often as you exercise rigor and severity, it is wholly owing to their idleness and obstinacy. By these means, you will open their hearts to instruction and prepare them to receive the truth of the Gospel … that you may be found in that number at the great Day of Accounts, is the sincere desire and earnest prayer of your faithful servant, Edm.[12]

What an admonition! We do not know how much of this was carried out by the slave masters. We do know what was expected of the clergy.

Some Africans perceived this intention of the church to receive instruction in the Christian faith. Within their area of enslavement, they became acquainted with the Anglican clergy and expressed their desire to receive the Christian Sacrament of Baptism. What stands out is how persistent these Africans were over time and over space to seek out Anglican Christianity.

Here is a sample from the SPG archive:

In a 1733 request to London for help, the writer said, "…that [Mr. Flint Dwight] be appointed catechist for the Parish of Rye with liberty of teaching school in such places of the Parish where he may have a prospect of being most service and particularly that he should also instruct the Negroes … he should have the opportunity to instruct the Negroes, as well as the white children. … that he should instruct and catechize the Negroes, as well as teach the white children. The society have also ordered you 200 catechisms and 30 Common Prayers with singing Psalms."[13]

---

12 David Humpheys, *An Historical Account of the Incorporated Society for the Propagation of the Gospel in Foreign Parts …to the year 1728* (London, 1730), pages 269-270.

13 *Society for Propagation of the Gospel, [December 21, 1733, a London Letter from David Humphrey to Rev Whitmore, Rye, NY. [C Series Box 12 item 64]*

The geographic scope of this mission in one year:

From St. Paul's Parish in South Carolina on September 29, 1746, the Rev. William Orr reported, "I am preparing some adult negroes for the Sacrament of Baptism, a work of no small labor and difficulty, considering the aversion which many of their owners have to such a thing."[14]

- In North Carolina, on April 19, 1747, the Rev. Clement Hall reported Black baptisms: eleven children and five adults.[15]
- In New York, July 16, 1747, Joseph Mildreth noted twelve negroes attended school in the evening.[16]
- Again, in New York, in New Rochelle, July 1747, the Rev. Strouppe recorded he baptized 15 children, Black and white.[17]

In a single year, the Rev. William Ayers in Freehold, New Jersey, reported:

On September 30, 1771, "[I]t being inconvenient for them to attend in the winter, on Sundays between the Morning and Evening prayer; and likewise the Negroes, Men, Women, and children, belonging to my people on the same seasons and days in the afternoon."[18]
On May 12, 1772, "I have baptized thirteen infants, four of them Blacks."[19]

---

14   SPG Archives. B Series Vol 15, September 29, 1746.
15   SPG Archives. B Series Vol 15, April 19, 1747.
16   Ibid, 148.
17   Ibid, 151.
18   SPG Archives. B Series Vol 15, September 30, 1771
19   SPG Archives. B Series Vol 15, May 12, 1772

On September 29, 1772, and April 10, 1774, "I continue to officiate in each part of my mission: in performing Divine Service, catechizing the children of my hearers, and after evening Prayer instructing their Negroes, Men, women, and children."[20]

Over a dozen years, the Rev. Isaac Browne in Newark, New Jersey, reported his statistics:

- April 6, 1759: "I have christened 12 infants, two of which were black."[21]

- January 6, 1760: "Christened 51 infants – 7 of which were black."[22]

- April 1760: "Christened 13 white infants and 1 black."[23]

- October 6, 1760: "Christened 24 white infants and 2 Negro children."[24]

- October 1762: "Christened 26 infants of which 5 were Negroes."[25]

- April 4, 1764: "Christened 24 white infants, 6 blacks; 5 white adults and 1 black adult."[26]

- October 6, 1764: "Christened 18 infants and 4 adults of which one was a Negro man."[27]

- April 6, 1771: "Christened 11 infants of which 3 were Negro children."[28]

20 *SPG Archives*. B Series Vol 15, September 29, 1772, April 10, 1774

21 *SPG Archives*. B Series Vol 15, April 6, 1759.

22 *SPG Archives*. B Series Vol 15, January 6, 1760.

23 *SPG Archives*. B Series Vol 15, April 1760.

24 *SPG Archives*. B Series Vol 15, October 6, 1760.

25 *SPG Archives*. B Series Vol 15, October 1762.

26 *SPG Archives*. B Series Vol 15, April 4, 1764.

27 *SPG Archives*. B Series Vol 15, October 6, 1764.

28 *PG Archives*. B Series Vol 15, April 6, 1771.

- October 6, 1771: Browne stated he had completed 28 years as a missionary in New Jersey and was the longest-serving clergyman in that area. He christened nine infants and 1 Black.[29]

From Lewes, Delaware, the Rev. Arthur Usher wrote to London on September 29, 1743, "I have since baptized fifteen children and two adults, one of them mulatto, before I baptized her, could say her prayers and repeat the church catechism."[30]

As early as 1713, Mrs. Haige and Mrs. Edwards of South Carolina took it upon themselves to go to a plantation and teach Africans the Principles of the Christian religion. They met with them over six months, with fourteen Africans desiring baptism, which Rev. Taylor administered on the Lord's Day.[31]

On September 30, 1743, the Rev. Richard Charlton of New York wrote: "My poor Negroe Catechumens shew'd a deep concern at the time of my extreme illness. ... Eighteen Negroes have been baptized."[32] *The Negro History Journal* notes his baptizing two hundred nineteen slaves from 1732 to 1740.[33]

In Hanover County, Virginia, Rev. Samuel Davies, a Presbyterian, wrote to John Wesley in 1755 that he had about three hundred Africans attending his services, out of which one hundred were instructed in the faith and baptized. He mentioned the congregation next door had the same number under his care.[34]

29　*SPG Archives*. B Series Vol 15, October 6, 1771

30　*SPG Archives*. B Series Vol 15, September 29, 1743.

31　David Humpheys, *An Historical Account of the Incorporated Society for the Propagation of the Gospel in Foreign Parts...to the year 1728* (London, 1730), page 246.

32　*SPG Archives*. B Series Vol 15, September 30, 1743

33　C.E. Pierre, *The Journal of Negro History,* Vol 1, No. 4 (Oct. 1916), page 358.

34　*Works of John Wesley,* Vol. 21 (July 27, 1755, pages 21-22.

The Rev. Mr. Auchmutty, who served from 1747 to 1764, reported that there was among the Africans an ever-increasing desire for instruction and "not one single Black" that had been "admitted by him to the Holy Communion" had "turned out bad or been in any shape a disgrace to our holy Profession."[35]

On October 28, 1769, the Rev. James Macartney of Granville County, North Carolina, wrote that he had baptized two hundred twenty-one whites and seventy-nine Blacks.[36]

These records illustrate the intensive ministry to catechize and baptize Africans who lived under very demanding and restricted circumstances in their time.

The reason later generations have not understood the wide scope of this ministry[37] is that it became commonplace to suppress the record of actual Black baptisms. Transcriber John Vogt of Bruton Parish in Williamsburg, Virginia, has noted that the birth and baptismal records for the period 1662-1797 omitted two thousand names of slaves from an earlier published account.[38] Delaware Episcopal historian Nelson Waite Rightmyer estimated that there were at least five hundred baptisms omitted in Delaware.[39] The number could be higher since he admitted he did not actually counted them. In Dover, Delaware, Mr. Neill baptized as many as one hundred sixty-two Negroes (One hundred

---

35 Ibid.

36 *SPG Archives*. B Series Vol 5, October 28, 1769.

37 Thomas, James S. *Methodism's Racial Dilemma* (Nashville: Abingdon Press, 1992), page 23.

38 *Bruton Parish, Virginia 1662-1797*. Transcribed & edited by John Vogt. New Papyrus Publishing Co: Athens, Georgia. 2004. Page iii

39 Nelson Waite Rightmyer, *The Anglican Church in Delaware* (Philadelphia: The Church Historical Society, 1947), page 162.

forty-five being adult slaves) within eighteen months.[40] Colonial history scholar Patricia Bonomi found that in just two Virginia parishes, five hundred fifty-four slaves had been baptized by 1732. Between 1740-1775, in Albemarle Parish, eight hundred forty-six baptisms were administered to slaves.[41] She has revised her understanding that only a few Blacks were interested in being Christian before the Second Great Awakening.[42]

During his Georgia missionary adventure,[43] John Wesley, later the leader of Methodism, observed the work of the Anglican SPG among the African slaves[44] and recorded his experiences in his Journal:

1. Monday, August 1736.

I set out for Lieutenant—Governor's seat, about thirty miles from Charleston, to deliver Mr. Oglethorpe's letters. It stands very pleasantly on a little hill, with a vale on either side, in one of which is a thick wood; the other is planted with rice and Indian corn. I designed to have gone back by Mr. Skene's, who has about fifty Christian Negroes. But my horse tiring, I was obliged to return the straight way to Charleston.[45] This corroborated David Humphreys' account in 1730:

---

40   Charles Frederick Pascoe, *Two hundred years of the S.P.G.: an historical account of the Society For The Propagation Of The Gospel In Foreign Parts, 1701-1900* (Based on a digest of the Society's records) (London: Pub. At Society's Office, 1901), page 39.

41   Patricia U. Bonomi, *Under the Cope of Heaven: Religion, Society, and Poltics in Colonial America* (updated Edition), (Oxford: Oxford Press, 1986, 2003), vii-xi.

42   Patricia U. Bonomi, *Journal of American History*, "Swarms of Negroes Comeing about My Door": Black Christianity in Early Dutch and English North America, June 2016

43   The Georgia Colony was the Society for the Propagation of Christian Knowledge's (SPCK). Its efforts for prison reform consisted of having convicts move from England to Georgia. The Wesleys, John as Chaplain and Charles as secretary, joined General James Oglethorpe's team.

44   Georgia did not have slavery. He observed slavery when in South Carolina.

45   *The Works of John Wesley*, Vol. 18, Journals and Diaries 1 (1735-1738) pp. 169-170. [Footnote 29 on page 170].

"The Clergy of South Carolina did, in a joint letter to the Society, after a representation made of the state of the Church there, acquaint them, that Mr. Skeen, his lady, and Mrs. Haige, his sister, did use great care to have their negroes instructed and baptized. And the Rev. Mr. Vamod, missionary in that Parish, did, at the same time, write to the Society, that he had baptized in the foregoing year, eight negro children, belonging to Mr. Skeen and Mrs. Haige, who, he says, "took great pains to have their slaves instructed in our faith, and that, at once, he had nineteen negroes communicants."

Humphreys added that Alexander Skene, a wealthy landowner from Barbados, was one of the councilmen of South Carolina. He was the first planter to agree to the attempted conversion of his slaves by the SPG missionaries in 1715.[46]

2. Saturday, April 23, 1737.

. . . He (Mr. Thompson, minister of St. Bartholomew's, near Ponpon) went with me twenty miles, and sent his servant to guide me the other twenty miles to his house. Finding a young Negro there, who seemed more sensible than the rest, I asked her how long she had been in Carolina. She said two or three years; but had been born in Barbados and had lived there in a minster's family from a child. I asked whether she went to church there.

She said, "Yes, every Sunday—to carry my mistress's children."

I asked what she had learned at church.

She said, "Nothing: I heard a deal, but did not understand it."

"But what did your master teach you at home?"

---

46 David Humphreys, *Historic Account of the Incorporated Society for the Propagation of the Gospel in Foreign Parts.* London. MDCCXXX 1730 and footnote 29 on page 170.

"Nothing."

"Not your mistress?"

"No."

I asked, "But don't you know that your hands and feet, and this you call your body, will turn to dust in a little time?"

She answered, "Yes."

"But there is something in you that will not turn to dust, and this is what they call your soul. Indeed, you can't see your soul, though it is within you, as you can't see the wind, though it is all about you. But if you had not a soul in you, you could no more see, or hear, or feel, than this table can. What do you think will become of your soul, when your body turns to dust?"

"I don't know."

"Why, it will go out of your body and go up there, above the sky, and live always. God lived there. Do you know who God is?"

You can't see him, any more than you can see your own soul. It is he that made you and me, and all men and women, and all beasts and birds, and all the world. It is he that makes the sun shine and rain fall, and corn and fruits to grow out of the ground. He makes all these for us. But why do you think he made us, what did he make you and me for?"

"I can't tell."

"He made you to live with himself above the sky. And so you will, in a little time—if you are good. If you are good, when your body dies your soul will go up, and want nothing, and have whatever you can desire. No one will beat or hurt you there. You will never be sick. You will never be sorry any more, nor afraid of anything. I can't tell you, I don't know, how happy you will be; for you will be with God."

The attention with which this poor creature listened to instruction is inexpressible. The next day she remembered all, readily answered every question, and said she would ask him that made her to show her how to be good.[47]

3. Wednesday, April 27, 1737.

... "Mr. Bellinger sent a Negro lad with me to Purrysburg (a township up the Savannah River), or rather to the poor remains of it. O how hath God stretched over this place 'the lines of confusion and the stones of emptiness!' (Isaiah 34:11) Alas for those whose lives were here vilely cast away, through oppression, through divers plaques and troubles! O earth! How long wilt thou hide their blood! How long wilt thou cover thy slain? (Isaiah 26:21)

"This lad too I found both very desirous and very capable of instruction. And perhaps one of the easiest and shortest ways to instruct the American Negroes in Christianity would be first to inquire after and find out some of the most serious planters. Then, having inquired of them which of their slaves *were best inclined,* and understood English, to go to them from plantation to plantation, staying so long as appeared necessary at each. Three or four gentlemen in Carolina I have been with that would be sincerely glad of such an assistant, who might pursue his work with no more hindrances than must everywhere attend the preaching of the gospel."[48] Twenty-one years later, Wesley baptised two

---

47 *The Works of John Wesley,* Vol. 18, pp. 179-180.

48 *The Works of John Wesley,* Vol. 18, page, 181.

Negroes' belonging to Nathaniel Gilbert on Wednesday, November 29, 1758. Wesley commented on the female servant: "The first African Christian I have known . . ."[49]

Looking over the whole sweep of the colonial period, Africans responded to Anglican Christianity year after year by the hundreds, which totaled into the thousands all across British North America in spite of resistance by most of the enslavers. Africans sought the education they wanted for Christian baptism.

---

49   Henry D. Rack, *Reasonable Enthusiast: John Wesley and the Rise of Methodism* (Philadelphia: Trinity Press International, 1989), p. 477. The Negroes may have been from Antigua. By 1773 two-thirds of the sixty Antigua Methodists were Black.

CHAPTER 4

African Americans Find Anglican Christianity Through Education

D r. Bray established the Society for Promoting Christian Knowledge (SPCK) in 1724 to provide books and libraries for the colonial clergy and the ministry of the church. Later, the SPCK adopted the program of prison reform of sending convicts to the Colony of Georgia. After he died in 1730, Dr. Bray's associates continued his legacy of education by establishing schools for slaves, known as Bray Schools. All of these endeavors - SPG, SPCK, and Bray Associate Schools - were in cooperation and reinforced each other's mission.

Elias Neau, in New York City, led the most successful school, which had a large population of slaves. He used funding from the Society for the Propagation of the Gospel in 1704 to start a school for enslaved persons. Guided by his love and connection to the Book of Common Prayer, Neau, a Huguenot (French Protestant), became a member of Trinity Church and served on its Vestry from 1705 to 1713.

In partnership with Trinity's first rector, the Rev. William Vesey, Neau and his students convened in Trinity Church's steeple on Wednesdays, Fridays, and Sundays. The Rev. Vesey would also teach and baptize those who wished to enter the faith. Before Neau died in 1722, and in less than ten years, Neau had two hundred pupils. The Vestry minutes of Trinity Church reported that a considerable number. . . of [1,400 slaves] by the Society's charity have already been instructed in the principles of Christianity and received Holy Baptism. They are communicants and frequently approach the altars.

Trinity Church and other teachers continued Neau's life's work. In 1788, the first of many African Free Schools was established by the Manumission Society of New York on land donated by Trinity. Each year, The Episcopal Church honors Elias Neau on September 7 for his dedicated ministry.[50]

In 1743, in Charleston, South Carolina, the SPG paid to have two Black youths, Harry and Andrew, to be trained as teachers for a school for African Americans. This establishment was a training school for bright young Blacks who felt called to instruct their fellow countrymen. Africans teaching Africans. There were fifty-five children in the day school, and in the evening school were fifteen adults who came after a hard day's work. The program lasted

---

50   Jewels Tauzin, 'trinitywallstreet.org.' "Points of Interest: Elias Neau and Trinity's Outreach to Native Americans and the Enslaved," September 3, 2021. Bonomi, *Under the Cope of Heaven,* page ix. C. E. Pierre, *The Work of the Society of the Propagation of the Gospel in Foreign Parts Among the Negroes in the Colonies* (Washington: *Journal of Negro History,* 1916). Digital copy.

twenty years. In 1763, for some unknown reason, the institution was closed, although it was the only educational institution for 50,000 Blacks.[51]

In 1755, the Georgia Society for the Propagation of the Gospel hired a catechist schoolmaster for Negroes.[52] At that time, Mr. Joseph Ottlenghi was sent to be a catechist and schoolmaster to the Negro children in the colony of Georgia. His letters on his work never reached London, he says, because the French and Indian War interrupted the ships carrying his report. During his time, he recounts that Georgia was organized into parishes to be served by the Church of England.[53]

At the suggestion of Benjamin Franklin, a school was established in Philadelphia. It operated until the second year of the Revolution and reopened in 1786. It could have been possible for the slave who wrote a letter to Joseph Pilmore in 1771 to have been educated at the school. The Philadelphia school operated until 1845.

Bray Associate Schools were established in Newport, Rhode Island (1762-1776), Williamsburg (1760-1774) and Fredericksburg, Virginia (1765-1770). The Williamsburg school had thirty-three students (nineteen boys, fourteen girls) in 1764.[54]

---

51   Colyer Meriwether, and Edward McCrady, *History of Higher Education in South Carolina* (Washington: Government Press, 1889), page 123. Frederick Dalcho, *An Historical Account of the Protestant Episcopal Church in South Carolina* (Charleston: E. Thayer, 1820), 156, 158, 164

52   *SPG Archives,* "Letter" 15 January 1759.

53   *SPG Archives,* "Letter by Joseph Ottlenghi," *C Series, Box 8, No. 1 item.*

54   *Encyclopedia Virginia* online. "Associates of Dr. Bray and the Bray Schools."

The structural foundation on which Black Methodism is built is hard to see today. The Society for the Propagation of the Gospel built a solid foundation on which African-American Methodism would be constructed. While the enslavers were opposed to their African slaves desire for education, that did not stop the slaves from seeking an education. We may never know how many wanted to read and write but were stopped. What is known is that against tremendous odds Africans sought an education.

CHAPTER 5

Africans Respond to Whitefield's Methodism

While the Society for the Propagation of the Gospel worked across the colonies, Rev. George Whitefield landed in Lewes, Delaware in 1739. From his youth, Whitefield demonstrated his gift as a mesmerizing preacher to crowds of thousands. His impact cannot be overstated on colonial Americans and on Africans who joined his Methodist-style societies.

His spiritual story began as a student at Oxford University. Whitefield was invited by Charles Wesley to the Holy Club, founded by Charles Wesley and his brother John. Later, when the Wesley brothers were ministering in Georgia, he became the leader of the Holy Club, at the time the center of Methodism in England. Whitefield had founded the first Methodist society in England and was the first leader of the group that became known as the "Methodists." When the Wesleys returned, Whitefield introduced John to the radical practice of field preaching outside the confines of the church sanctuary.

As Whitefield prepared to sail for America, he returned the leadership of the Methodist work to his elder Anglican minister, John Wesley. Both men needed their own area of ministry: Colonial America became Whitefield's focus, and Wesley's the United Kingdom.

With his reputation preceding him to America, Whitefield was invited to preach to the people of Lewes. Out of that experience, the first Methodist society was founded in America. The negative response becomes the first of what will be commonplace throughout his preaching up and down the East Coast. The first evidence of this push back is an angry letter by the Anglican minister, the Rev. William Becket, to Governor Thomas on January 2, 1741:

> 'Tho' my churches are full as ever. Yet Mr. Whitefield has dropt some of his Enthusiastic venom at Lewes. I have not been there this fortnight, the Weather is so bad. But they have set up a Society in my absence. I ask'd the man that told me this what was the meaning of a Society. He told me they were to meet to sing Psalms & Hymns &c twice a week. There is no harm in the Affair, if there by no counter plot. But I cannot forbear suspecting that Whitefield & Tools have laid Schemes all over America, to draw people to dislike of our Church Doctrine Discipline & Government...'[55]

---

55 Rightmyer, (Becket Letter to Governor Thomas, January 2, 1741) 116. Whitefield visited Lewes again in May 1740.

Again, on April 25, 1741, Becket wrote to Commissary Commings:

It is surprising to observe how the vulgar, everywhere are inclined to Enthusiasm. Mr. Whitefield had a vast crowd of hearers at services in May last, where he preached 4 or 5 times from a balcony. I believe some times to (grot cess?) than 14 or 1500 of all sorts. They had tried unknown to me to set up a Religious Society. Some of the church people (a few for they made up not above 30 of all sorts) joined them, but still they came to Church on Sunday. Holidays: by using them with Moderation prevails with those that used to receive the Sacrament not to break Church communion, so they rec'd on Easter Sunday. But this Humour of theirs seems like all other violent things not to be of long continuance, for they are dropping from one another both here and elsewhere thro' this Province, as I am informed. God only knows what may be the issue of these things at last. We can only trust in God & do our duty.[56]

In spite of his hope that this "enthusiasm" would diminish, the Methodists were still meeting in 1751:

...I have baptized 18 white children, 2 Negro children, and 1 adult white woman, after previous examination ... my congregations daily increase, notwithstanding, efforts of the Methodists, to Disturb the peace of the Church. They seem rigid, but now, when they have not one of their own let (me) preach to them, they constantly come to Church, which makes me entertain some hope,

---

56   *SPG Archives* Letter. April 25, 1741. Rev. Becket writes to the Philadelphia Commissary Cummings. Transcribed by author from the original.

that they will in God's due time unite with us at Lewes Church on Christmas Day..."[57]

Becket's correspondence reveals the tension that existed between the Methodist revival with its enthusiastic response and the established Anglican order. Lewes Methodists gathered continuously for over twenty years before John Street Church was built in New York.

After landing in Lewes in 1739, Whitefield preached in Philadelphia, where he met the eminent colonial statesman, Benjamin Franklin. After hearing him preach, Franklin offered to publish his sermons. As part of his evangelistic follow—up mission, Whitefield founded small groups that included African American members. The breadth of his mission is evident in his April 28, 1740, correspondence to a Mr. M. in New Brunswick, New Jersey, just a few months after landing in America:

In short, the word hath run and been much glorified; and many Negroes also are in a fair way of being brought home to God . . . Bring your Indian hearers to believe, before you talk of baptism, or the supper of the Lord.[58]

In his Journal entry for May 11, 1740, about two weeks later, he gives a more complete picture:

Nearly fifty Negroes came to give me thanks for what God had done to their souls. How heartily did those poor creatures throw in their mites (small donation for his Georgia orphanage) for

---

57 *SPG Archives.* "Letter." April 25, 1741. Rev Arthur Ussher, Lewes to SPG London (transcribed by author from original) Ten years after Becket's letter!

58 George Whitefield, *Letters of George Whitefield, for the Period 1734-1742* [Kindle Locations 3175-3176]. Banner of Truth Trust. Kindle Edition.

my poor orphans. Some of them have begun to learn to read. One, who was free, said she would give me her two children, whenever I settle my school … I intended, had time permitted, to have settled a Society[59] for Negro men and Negro women; but that must be deferred till it shall please God to bring me to Philadelphia again. I have been much drawn out in prayer for them, and have seen them exceedingly wrought upon under the Word preached . . .[60]

From Reedy Island near Lewes, he wrote a letter, again less than two weeks later, on May 22, 1740, to a Mr. R. Affectionately, he commends himself to a Black Philadelphia woman named Peggy and asks for her prayers:

LET nothing said to you in my absence affect you. God has lately delivered you out of one snare; take heed how you fall into another. If you watch unto prayer, who knows but God may bless your endeavors amongst the poor negro women and children? I could not wish you more happily situated.— My love to all the society.— Exhort them not to rest in good desires. Shew them, O shew them the necessity of being deeply wounded, before they can be capable of healing by Jesus Christ. Bid them to beware of a light behavior, and light company. Both do grieve the blessed spirit of God; Take heed, take heed of those accursed snares. I could say more, but time will not permit. My love to the Negro Peggy, and all her black sisters. Bid them to pray for me. May the blood of Jesus wash away all the pollution of their sin-sick souls! What if they were put into a

---

59 *At least twenty-six societies began in the city as a result of the revivals. Kidd, Thomas S. George Whitefield: America's Spiritual Founding Father, (New Haven: Yale University Press, 2014), p. 115.*

60 *Whitefield, Journal, 274.*

society by themselves, and you, or some white woman, meet with them? The good Lord direct and bless you in all things.— This is the hearty prayer of LETTER. Your sincere friend and fervent in Christ, G.[61]

The tantalizing question is: Where did the descendants of Whitefield's ministry in Philadelphia find their spiritual home? Since Whitefield was Anglican, did some later join St. Thomas Episcopal Church? Was a motivation for Richard Allen to build Bethel Church outside the Methodist Episcopal Church to attract those White-field Africans who may or may not have associated themselves with St. Georges Church? Several decades after Rev. George Whitefield's death, a Black family in Kentucky named their son George C. White-field,[62] who later served Mother Bethel AME Church. Was his family descendants of these Blacks who wanted to show their spiritual lineage went back to Whitefield? More importantly, is 1740 in Philadelphia the beginning of African Methodism in America?

Whitefield wrote on the same day to Mr. G. L. in London from Reedy Island, as he awaited a boat to take him to Georgia, the location of his main mission, the Orphans' House in Georgia. The following was an advertisement to be printed in England to help him continue to gain support for the House:

Mr. Whitefield went on board at New Castle, in order to sail to Georgia after having been on shore thirty-three days, and travelled some hundreds of miles, and preached fifty-eight times in

61   Whitefield, Letter *CL XXXVI*. To Mr. R, at Philadelphia. Dear R. Reedy Island, May 22, 1740.

62   Alexander W. Wayman, *Cyclopedia of African Methodism*, p. 180.

the provinces of New Jersey, New York, and Pennsylvania. His congregations consisted sometimes of four, sometimes of five, sometimes of eight, twelve, fifteen, and once at Philadelphia of twenty thousand people. He had gotten near five hundred pounds sterling, in money and provisions, for the Orphan house at Georgia. Great and visible effects followed his preaching, almost wheresoever he went, especially in Philadelphia. There was never such a general awakening, and concern for the things of God known in America before. He intended to visit New—England soon after his arrival at Georgia, and to come by land as far as Philadelphia, at the latter end of the year.

Whitefield continued:

The above Advertisement may suffice for the present, 'till I have an opportunity of sending you my journal. . . I hope there is a door opening among the Allegheny Indians. . . We have been near a week at Reedy Island: I have preached there five times. The captains and their crews come constantly to public worship on shore, and to private prayer in our sloop. We have some with us that love our dear Lord Jesus in sincerity. My heart is exceedingly drawn towards Savannah; but the Lord's time is the best. The Lord Jesus bless you all, and reward you for all kindnesses shewn to his unworthy servant, but Your affectionate brother in Christ, G.'[63]

In another letter, he wrote of his desire to visit New England. As in Lewes, the local Anglican clergy held a dim view of his preaching and described it with alarm. Yet, the letter reveals the similar effect his

---

63 Whitefield, *Letter CC.*

preaching had on people in Boston. Roger Price wrote to his SPG superiors in London on January 29, 1742:

> Our whole attention is now taken up with the strange affairs produced by the new doctrines lately revived by Mr. Whitefield in these parts, and industriously propagated by his followers since, by whole labours they are become almost universal; his madness prevails chiefly in the country towns tho' there are many appearances of it in Boston, and no pains working to excite it. The Church of England has escaped beyond our expectation, but we are not without our fear and danger. The enclosed is the exactest account I could procure of this affair and well agrees with common report. You will from hence be able to judge what assistance we stand in most need of from the writings of the learned at Home, what we have already records has had its intended effect, and a renewal of the Societies bounty, as they shall judge most suitable will be very seasonable and thankfully accepted. I am your most obedient humble servant, Roger.[64]

From Boston, around the same time as the perceived turmoil in Lewes, Rev. Timothy Cutler wrote on June 26, 1750, to the SPG leaders and included his regular report. With a key emphasis on the SPG mission directed toward slaves, Cutler reported his record of baptisms. Like others before him, he expressed his displeasure with the Methodists. His account provides evidence of the continued Methodist presence begun by Whitefield that continued as a "small congregation," which may have been a Methodist society:

---

64   *SPG Archives.* "Letter." Roger Price. January 29, 1742, from Boston to London SPG (transcribed by the author from the original).

I have baptized 20 persons & whereof are Negro children, and one of them a slave … Another a Negro Woman, who expressed herself very sensibly and well—disposed to her Duty … There are ten (?) Independent Congregations, and a small one sprung from Methodism…The Confusions of Methodism are not over, and do in a special sad manner affect the Peace and Quietness of some of our Country Towns, where Methodism multiplies its shapes, and those very awful and deformed ones too. Some make a good use of these things: but with too many they are an Argument against Religion, and Introductory of Skepticism, Infidelity and Perfidy.[65]

The emotional impact of Whitefield's ministry was long-lasting, as Joseph Pilmore testified in his August 13, 1771, Journal entry:

Immediately upon my arrival at home my housekeeper told me of the death of my ever Dear and venerable Friend, Mr. Edward Evans. He was savingly converted to God about thirty years ago under the ministry of that precious man of God, Mr. Whitefield and has maintained an unspotted character from the beginning. When Providence brought Mr. Boardman and me to America, he united with us most heartily, and was made a most useful instrument amongst us. As he frequently went into the Jerseys to preach, the people were exceedingly fond of him, built a pretty chapel, and insisted on having him for their Minister. After he had been with them a few months he took the fall—fever which soon brought him to his grave.[66]

---

65 *SPG Archives.* "Letter." Rev. Timothy Cutler. From Boston To London. June 26, 1750. (transcribed by the author from the original) Pilmore, *Journal,* August 13, 1771.

66 Pilmore, *Journal,* August 13, 1771.

Pilmore had met Whitefield in England and had gotten advice from him about America. After both of them arrived in the colonies, Pilmore wrote affectionately about him, and shortly thereafter, Whitefield died. He expressed great feelings for him.[67]

The first African-American poet was Phyllis, a servant girl of seventeen years of age, belonging to Mr. J. Wheatley of Boston. She is known to us as Phyllis Wheatley. She had been in America for nine years from Africa. His death so moved her that she wrote: "An Elegiac Poem on the Death of that celebrated Divine, and Eminent Servant of Jesus Christ, the Reverend and learned George Whitefield." It was printed and sold by Ezekial Russell and John Boyles in Boston in 1770.

Later, the American circuit rider, Freeborn Garrettson, noted in his diary about Whitefield's ministry and its impact. He wrote that the first Methodist structure in America was the Georgia Orphan & Academy.[68]

. . . . and "by the multitudes of people, old and young, rich and poor, flocking to the churches . . .Garrettson continued: "A taste for experimental religion had, it is true, been created in some hearts, by the powerful preaching of the celebrated Whitefield, who, sometime previously to the arrival of the Methodist missionaries, had travelled through the country, and preached with his usual and success . . .[69]

---

67 Pilmore, 23.
68 Bangs, *Garrettson,* Introduction.
69 Bangs, *Garrettson,* 15, 76

Eight years after Whitefield's death, Garrettson described the enduring impact of Whitefield's preaching:

September 12th, 1778, was the first day of my entering the town of Dover ... Mr. Pryor, a merchant, who was formerly awakened under Mr. Whitefield . . . I preached at a place Quantico, Maryland, and a similar work broke there. The Lord raised a society, and many souls were converted; among others, old sister Rider, who was formerly a hearer of Mr. Whitefield . . . Old Mr. and Mrs. Rider . . . advanced toward me in tears, and the old lady spoke as follows: 'Many years ago we heard Mr. Whitefield preach, and we were brought to taste the sweetness of religion.[70]

George Whitefield was the only Methodist from England to preach in all the colonies until the 1760s. As is evident in these letters, African Americans and Native Americans were a focus of his ministry. He had bought land in Nazareth, Pennsylvania, to establish a future community of freed African slaves to be free to order their lives as they saw fit. His vision was greater than his resources, and he eventually sold it to the Moravians.

What Whitefield's Methodist message of the new birth gave to the enslaved Africans was a new way of understanding themselves. Being born again was a new identity the Africans embraced—no longer a slave but now a child of God. That new identity was strengthened by frequent gatherings with other Africans and whites in a society of new birth people. In this setting of singing and praying, they could experience the movement of God.

---

70 Bangs, *Garrettson*, 82.

The handing of the American baton from Whitefield's African American ministry to Wesley's British connectional system was in the person of Francis Asbury. As Asbury settled into his new environment, he learned how to adapt Wesley's system to the realities of the feisty Americans and the established Church of England. He poured African American Methodists into this transformative system of American Wesleyan Methodism.

CHAPTER 6

How Colonial Methodism Functioned: Two Peas in a Pod

Since the American colonies were part of the British Empire, the Church of England was the established church. John Wesley crafted British Methodism to function as part of the Church of England and not as a separate Dissenter church. This allowed him to avoid the prohibitions Parliament had put on Dissenter churches and clergy and released him from having to pay Dissenter fees to operate outside the Church of England. Along with his Arminian theology, he had distanced himself from the Reformed Dissenters and moved closer to Roman Catholic theology while remaining within the Church of England.

The image of 'two peas in a pod' captures Wesley's relationship with the state religion. Peas share the same life source in the pod while being unique in and of themselves. The pod is necessary for the peas to become fruitful. The pod is Anglicanism with the Church of England as its institutional embodiment. The first pea was the Society for the

Propagation of the Gospel, a mission arm in her colonies that supported of the Church of England's congregations. The second pea was the lay renewal movement of Methodism.

Strictly speaking, neither group was an official organization of the Church of England. The SPG had closer ties to the Church of England through the Crown's relationship with the church. Anglican clergy took a vow of loyalty to the Crown, from which the SPG recruited its missionaries and financial support. Whereas Methodism understood itself as a lay renewal movement within the Church of England. Methodist preachers were lay and only needed Wesley's blessing to preach. The priest for Baptism and Holy Communion were under the control of Anglican clergy from whom Methodists received these Sacraments.

The focus of Methodist preachers was on a 'new-birth' conversion. They preached outside the church and not during Anglican worship services. The Methodist 'congregation' was whenever and wherever an audience could be gathered for the sermon. As people were spiritually awakened, they were to go to the local Anglican priest for the Sacraments of Baptism and Holy Communion.

The focus of Anglican clergy was preparing people to receive the Sacrament of Baptism. They dedicated significant time to teaching the Christian basics well enough for the inquirer to receive the Sacrament of Baptism. Both Methodist and SPG missionaries sought out slaves to experience God and learn about the Christian faith. Both worked toward the same goal of incorporating the unchurched into the Christian faith, while utilizing different approaches.

The relationship between the local Anglican church and the SPG was much closer than that of the Methodists. Methodists were often viewed as disrupters to the church's ministry and often brought the ire of the parish clergy. Since Methodists lacked the formal education to qualify for ordination, Anglican clergy did not see the Methodist lay preacher as his equal.

These tensions can be seen in Francis Asbury's relationship with three Delaware Anglican clergy. Asbury had a modest formal general education in England and no formal theological education; he was approved by John Wesley as a lay preacher. He did not have the status as a clergyman in the Church of England. The Delaware Anglican clergy were educated in America, but all three had to go to England for ordination:[71]

- **Magaw, Samuel;** Education: M.A., College of Philadelphia; Deacon; Priest: 15 February 1767, ordained at Chapel Royal at St. James's Palace.

- **Neill, Hugh**

  Deacon: 11 March; Priest:25 March 1749, ordained at the Church within the Temple precinct of London.

- **Thorn, Sidneyham;** Education: King's College, New York; Deacon, 21 August; Priest, 24 August 1774, ordained at Fulham Palace (Home of the Bishop of London).

- **Asbury, Francis**[72]

  English School to age 13. No College. 1784, ordained Deacon, Elder, and consecrated Bishop in Baltimore.

---

71 James B. Bell, American Antiquarian Society, "Anglican Clergy in Colonial America Ordained by Bishops of London," pp. 103-160.

72 John Wigger, *American Saint: Francis Asbury and the Methodists* (New York: Oxford University Press, 2009), p. 19.

In comparison to them, Asbury's general education was merger and his theological education was largely self-taught before his ordination and installation as bishop in 1784.

When Asbury started preaching in Delaware, the Anglican clergyman Samuel Magaw was upset with him doing religious services in his parish without his approval. After a while, Rev. Magaw realized Asbury would not be conducting sacramental services as a layperson. Relations improved when Asbury started attending his church and received Holy Communion from his hands.

On October 31, 1779, Asbury records:

We all went to church, preachers and people, and received the sacrament. Messrs. Thorn, O'Neal, and McGaw were present. Mr. O'Neal preached an affecting passion sermon, after the Lord's Supper Mr. McGaw preached an excellent sermon. At night I preached in the barn...[73]

Over time, Asbury. Magaw, Thorne, and Neill developed a mutual respect for each other that carried over into sharing ministry together. At the Methodist meeting house, known as Barratt's Chapel in Frederica, Delaware, the Anglican clergy conducted the first Holy Communion Service in the recently built building, with Asbury receiving the Sacrament from them.

On December 10, 1781, Francis Asbury attended Thorne's church . . . and on the twenty-first of the following January, Magaw and Thorne administered the communion at Barratt's Chapel: 'It was a gracious time, and I hope it will not be received in vain.'[74]

---

73 Nelson Waite Rightmyer, *The Anglican Church in Delaware* (Philadelphia: The Church Historical Society, 1947), page 118. Asbury's "Journal," October 31, 1779.

74 Rightmyer, 120 Asbury's "Journal," December 10, 1781.

Earlier, Asbury recorded how their relation worked between them:

I attended the communion; the communicants increased daily, for the people get awakened by us; when this is the case, they go to the Lord's Supper.[75]

Four years later, circumstances were altered with the Americans defeating Great Britain. John Wesley had ordained clergy for America and gave the Anglican Methodist, Rev. Thomas Coke, authority to ordain Asbury and to establish an American Methodist church. These English Methodist ambassadors met at Barratt's Chapel on November 14, 1784, for a Quarterly Conference. This marked the historic day when Methodists for the first time served the Sacraments in America. In the audience that day was the Rev. Magaw, who had been the officiant four years earlier. Asbury entered Barratt's Chapel with the service in progress, thinking it was improper for Methodists holding such a service, and was taken aback at first until he learned of the changes Wesley had authorized.[76] Now, major changes were felt all across American society. This was but one: the Anglican minister Magaw received the consecrated bread and the cup from a Methodist.

Methodists could grow their membership more easily than the Anglicans. One illustration was in 1780, the Methodists under Asbury could deploy eight men in Kent and Sussex Counties (Delaware) compared to the three Anglican priests.[77] This ability to

---

75   Rightmyer, 119. Quoted from Asbury's Journal, March 26, 1780.
76   Rightmyer, 120. (He has the incorrect month. It was November, not September, because according to Asbury's Journal, Coke was still in England in September)
77   Rightmyer, page 119.

deploy lay preachers may have influenced why so many African Americans joined Methodism after they had been baptized into the Church of England. As African-Americans were figuring out their spiritual lives in a hostile environment, they may have attended the priest's classes for baptism, however Anglican worship was from a prayer book. The Methodist preacher could gathered them with their friends into an oral, emotional, yet structured religious experience.

The interplay between the Anglicans and the Methodists is a key to understanding the development of African Methodism. It emerged from Anglicanism following the Revolutionary War, when the pod was no longer in America. These two peas developed each in their own way. A common heritage of the Anglican pod continued in each with the use of the name "Episcopal": Methodist Episcopal Church (in 1939 name changed to The Methodist Church) and the Protestant Episcopal Church.

ANGLICAN TRADITION [CHURCH OF ENGLAND] NORTH AMERICA

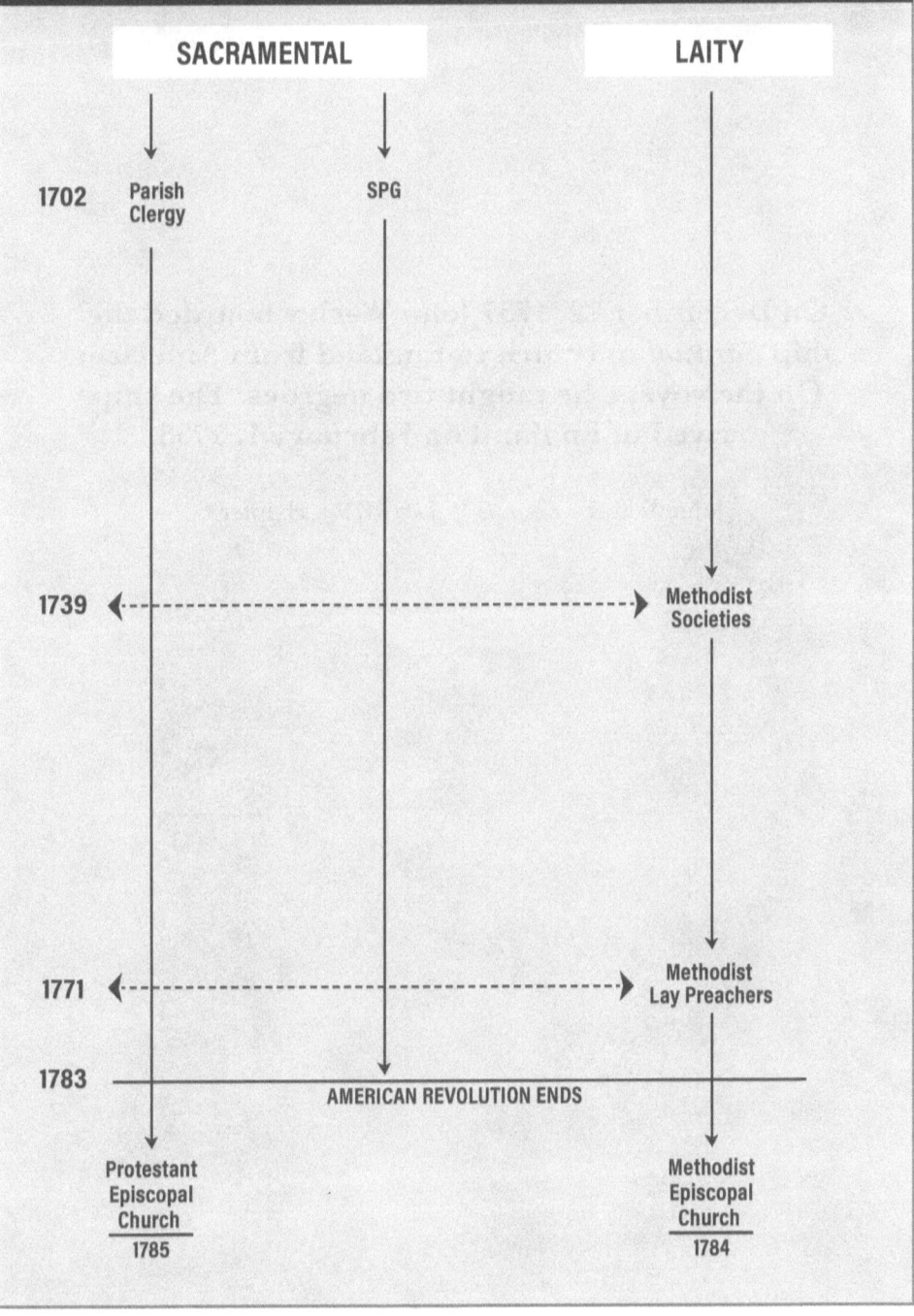

SACRAMENTAL		LAITY
Parish Clergy	SPG	
		Methodist Societies
		Methodist Lay Preachers

1702

1739

1771

1783 — AMERICAN REVOLUTION ENDS

Protestant Episcopal Church
1785

Methodist Episcopal Church
1784

On December 22, 1737 John Wesley boarded the ship *Samuel* to return to England from America. On the voyage he taught two negroes. The ship arrived in England on February 1, 1738.

John Telford, *The Life of John Wesley*, chapter 6.

CHAPTER 7

African Americans Embrace Wesley's Way

Africans embraced John Wesley's hymnal before he sent his missionaries to America. While Wesley lived in Georgia for two years, he published the *Collection of Psalms and Hymns* in 1737. Over time, he made further revisions to the collection. In 1755, a copy of one of his editions found its way into the hands of African Presbyterians in rural Virginia.

> Rev. Samuel Davies wrote to John Wesley about how Africans in the next congregation are "exceedingly delighted with Watt's Songs. . . . that the Negroes above all human species I ever knew, have the nicest ear for music. They have a kind of ecstatic delight in psalmody . . . (and) take so much pleasure in as those used in that heavenly part of divine worship.[78]

Though Wesley would never visit America again, African Americans were singing from his songbook!

---

78 Samuel Davies's (later President of Princeton) letter to John Wesley who quotes it in his Journal. WJW, Vol. 21. July 27, 1755, pages 21-22. John Todd was pastor he referenced using Wesley's hymnbook.

Ever since assuming the leadership of the Methodist movement in the British Isles from Whitefield, Wesley applied his full intellectual and personal strength for nearly thirty years to building the Wesleyan connectional system. The time came when American Methodists sought help from Wesley to send leaders to strengthen the American societies. Whitefield was the first to write him in September 1764 about the need for more Methodist preachers in the American colonies.[79] Early Methodist historian Jesse Lee claimed Whitefield had opened the way for later Methodist preachers to become leaders in the colonies.[80] As Wesley began to broach the possibility of his preachers coming to America, it was obvious that more help was needed, as Whitefield had been only one person and was now in poor health. He would die shortly after the first of Wesley's official missionaries arrived in Philadelphia in 1769.

Earlier, America was attracting other unofficially sent Methodists in the 1760s, such as Robert Williams, John King, Philip Embury, Barbara Heck, and others. Of these, the most notable was Robert Strawbridge and Captain Thomas Webb of the British military. Both men opened their ministry up to Africans wherever they preached. In 1767, Captain Webb wrote that when he preached in his own house "and several other places on Long Island," within six months, twenty—four people had been converted, "near half of them whites, the rest negroes."[81] Very possibly, the credit for the first African-Methodist preacher goes to Strawbridge. Jacob Toogood, a slave of John Maynard, was converted

79　*Armenian Magazine*, V (Aug., 1782), page 439. Quoted by Frank Baker, *From Wesley to Asbury*, page 26.

80　Jesse Lee, *A Short History of the Methodists*, page 38.

81　Captain Webb, 410.

under Strawbridge's ministry and given the responsibility of preaching to other Africans in the late 1760s.[82]

John Wesley's first official missionaries were Joseph Pilmore, who operated out of Philadelphia and Richard Boardman in New York. The presence of these Wesleyan preachers gave the opportunity for more Africans to have the experience of becoming 'born again' in the Methodist way. The Africans who attended the services of Captain Thomas Webb, Richard Boardman, and later Thomas Rankin in New York were probably slaves who were already baptized and knew the basic beliefs and practices of the Christian faith through the catechism classes conducted by Trinity Church and others. As Methodism grew, a Methodist meeting house, known initially as Wesley Chapel,[83] was built on John Street near Trinity Church. As the center of Methodism in the city, it became known later as John Street Methodist Church.

Meanwhile, Joseph Pilmore continued the Methodist practice of going to both Blacks and whites, as he wrote in his Journal:

Wednesday, September 5, 1770 - Philadelphia:

We met to gather to break bread. Our meeting was rather heavy and dull in the beginning: but we cried unto God, and he presently gave us his blessing of peace. Then people spoke freely of what he had done for their souls, and even poor Negroes came forth and bore noble testimony for God our Savior.[84]

---

82 George C. M. Roberts, Centenary Pictorial Album [1766-1866], Baltimore, J.W. Woods, 1866), page 28.

83 The African-American chapel in 1820 was known as Asbury.

84 Pilmore, Journal, page 51.

<u>Wednesday, August 5, 1772</u> – Norfolk, VA.:

> In the evening: After preaching two poor slaves came to me and begged I would instruct them in the way of salvation so I gave them a short and plain account of the Plan of the Gospel, and shewed them how sinners may come to God and be saved. We then joined in singing and prayer, and they expressed great thankfulness for what they had heard, and seemed determined to be Christians.[85]

<u>Sunday, August 9, 1772</u> – evening at Norfolk.

> As the ground was wet, they persuaded me to try to preach within and appointed men to stand at the doors to keep all the Negroes out till the White people were got in, but the house would not near hold them; I went into the pulpit; (and) began, but present a plank gave way, and the stage, on which the pulpit was fixed, began to sink down at one side, which so terrified the people that they cried out. As I perceived it would be impossible to quiet the people, I slipped out— ordered a Table and began singing in the large plain adjoining the house; this happened to be the very thing, the people drew out of the house, and I had a noble congregation of white and black, to whom I freely declared the whole counsel of God, and pressed them to obey the word of the Lord.'[86]

<u>Sunday, August 16, 1772,</u> Norfolk, Virginia, 7 p.m.

> "Yet we had the house perfectly [full] of white people, and a vast multitude of black people stood around about the outside."[87]

---

85 Pilmore, *Journal,* page 149
86 Ibid.
87 Ibid.

Then, in 1773, Wesley sent Thomas Rankin to be his assistant in superintending the missionaries in their work in America. Like those before him, he continued his outreach to Africans:

Sunday, July 4, 1773, We concluded with a general love feast. The people spoke with life and Divine blessing, and in particular some of the blacks.[88]

Monday, November 7, 1774 Deer Creek (Smyrna, Delaware) preparing for Quarterly Conference. At 10 a.m. the general love feast began. There was such a number of whites and blacks as never attended on such an occasion before. After we had sung and prayed . . . the power of the Lord descended in such an extraordinary manner . . . Near the close of our meeting I stood up . . . said 'See the number of the black Africans who have stretched out their hands and hearts to God![89]

From New York City in 1776:

The chapel was full of white and black, and many were without that could not get in. Look wherever we would, we saw nothing but streaming eyes, and faces bathed in tears; and heard nothing but groans and strong cries after God and the Lord Jesus Christ.[90]

Later, Bishop Hood wrote about the racially inclusive worship at John Street: "There were no Negro pews, no back seats, nor gallery especially provided for the dark-skinned members. We were welcome in common with other members to all the privileges of God's House of Worship.[91]

---

88 Thomas Rankin Journal as posted online: A I History Dunbar.
89 Thomas Rankin Journal as posted online: A I History Dunbar.
90 Thomas Rankin, 1776.
91 J.W. Hood, One Hundred Years of the African Methodist Episcopal Zion Church [1895], 203.

With the growth of Methodism and the return of English Methodist preachers and Anglican clergy to England because of the war, more American-born Methodists assumed leadership roles. The most significant was Freeborn Garrettson. As a Methodist, he was convinced that the right thing to do was to free his slaves and become a traveling preacher. To appreciate his compassion toward the enslaved, we read in his diary, as he records his feelings while traveling to the North Carolina Colony in September 1777:

> Many times did my heart ache on account of the slaves in this part of the country . . . I would often set apart times to preach to the blacks, and adapt my discourse to them alone; and precious moments have I had. While many of their sable faces were bedewed with tears, their withered hands of faith stretched out, and their precious souls made white in the blood of the Lamb. The suffering of these poor out casts of men, through the blessing of God, drove them near to the Lord and many of them were truly happy.[92]

On February 10, 1780, in Dorchester County, Maryland, Garrettson wrote:

> In the evening the family were gathered together for prayer. I shall never forget the time. I suppose about twelve white and black were present. The power of the Lord came among us. Mrs. Arey was so filled with the new wine of Christ's kingdom, that she sank to the floor, blessing and praising the Lord. And many of the blacks were much wrought upon.[93]

---

92 Nathan Bangs, *The Life of Freeborn Garrettson*, [New York, 1829], page 59. In Roanoke Chapel he preached to 500 whites and almost as many blacks, page 56.

93 Ibid, page 107.

In 1777, William Waters, the first Methodist to introduce Methodism to Talbot County, preached in Thomas Harrison's barn, west of St. Michaels, to both whites and Blacks.[94]

Later in 1804, the Talbot County Methodist preacher, the Rev. James Ridgway, recorded the following in his unpublished diary:

> I preached at the Line Chapel (west of Delmar, Delaware). We had a powerful time both in preaching and class meeting. At the close of the meeting I proposed to the people if any wanted to join to come forward. One black woman said. 'I want to join, but I dare not, my master won't let. He was as great an enemy to the Methodist as the devil could have.' He was present when she spoke and he rose up and said, 'Put her name down.' I askt him if he believed she had religion. He said he believed if she then died, she would go straight to heaven. This rejoiced my soul to hear that the blacks could preach to hardened masters.[95]

The Methodist Conference meeting at Baltimore in April 1780, four years before the 1784 Christmas Conference that institutionalized the Methodist movement as the Methodist Episcopal Church, asked in Question 25 of the session:

> Ought not the assistant meet with the colored people himself, and appoint as helpers in his absence proper white people and not suffer them to stay late and meet by themselves? . . . . Yes"[96]

---

94   Talbot Methodist File. Maryland Room. Talbot County Free Library, Easton, MD.

95   James Ridgway, *Diary*, Unpublished. August 5, 1804.

96   1780 *Conference Minutes*.

Jesse Lee, American Methodism's first historian, observed by 1773, there were enough Black Methodists to prompt him to write:

> Quarterly meetings moved from Tuesday to Saturday and Sunday .
> . . One weighty reason was that many of the slaves could not attend
> these meetings except on the Lord's Day.[97]

As these missionaries and American circuit riders took Wesley's system of societies and conferences out into the countryside, it only enhanced the Methodist outreach to Blacks and Blacks to Methodism, as Africans understood this system of spiritual oversight. It gave them the opportunity to become class leaders, exhorters, and local preachers. As Whitefield's ministry created the first American Methodists, Wesley's system created American Methodism.

---

97   Jesse Lee, *History of Methodism in America (1807)*, 1773.

CHAPTER 8

How American Methodism Functioned as a System

This chapter is about the unique mechanics of Methodism in America. The mature English Methodist system was developed by John Wesley after thirty years of development in the United Kingdom, before it was brought to the America colonies. The first English preachers from Whitefield on to America knew how the system worked within their experience. It had shaped them as laity into spiritual leaders. Methodism was both a message and a system designed to live out that message. The focus was on the spiritual development of the individual within the group to spread 'scriptural holiness throughout the land.' This philosophy was not a 'Jesus and me' Christianity. It was a 'Jesus, me, us, and the nation' tied together in one system.

The American landscape was longer and narrower than England and Wales. Though it was populated with a large number of African American slaves, its overall white population was much smaller than

Britian. Stretched along the coast, these thirteen separate colonies were loosely tied to one another and even less to the British monarch. Though John Wesley's principles of ministry were transferable to the colonies, how his system functioned had to be adapted to this new context.

The strength of Methodism in all its contexts was the class meeting (societies). They were open to whoever sought to be a Methodist. They lacked the barriers and status symbols of many religious movements. This allowed Blacks and whites living in the same area to develop a unique Methodist identity together.

To gain an appreciation of the Methodist ethos, consider Wesley's question: "Do you expect to be made perfect in love in this life?" Most modern American Methodists answer the question with a strong No! Wesley expected his Methodists to say YES! To him, if a person did not desire to seek that kind of love, that person did not want to be a Methodist. It takes little effort to point out that American Methodists did not fully experience that love transformation; however, relationships between Africans and whites were altered in these early Methodist societies. As the nation moved toward the Civil War, relationships between Blacks and whites did become more strained, and yet, they all still wanted to be known as Methodists!

The Methodist understanding of space was wherever a group could gather in a barn, carriage house, or under a tree. Methodism could function outside of a church building, unlike the Anglican Church or congregational life today. As a web of places and connections, it started within the community and not from a central location. It was a web of connections among people who met in whatever space was available for ministry. African Americans were not asked to enter a building unfamiliar

YEAR ▼	North America 'Colonies'	England & Wales 'Center of Power'
	Geography: East Coast (1,000 miles); Population in 1740: 900K	Geography: London to Scotland (400 mi.); Population in 1740: 6.1M
1736	**SOCIETIES** — George Whitefield's Innovations: Field Preaching, printing sermons; Developed classes; led Holy Club when JW in Georgia	**SOCIETIES** — Wesley followed Whitefield's innovations. JW develops "Holy Club" & first "Orphan's House"
1739	To America: Lewes, Delaware. First Society.	
1744	GW: New birth preaching. Establishing societies. Raise money for Georgia Orphan House. America is to spread out and population too sparse to build a national system.	
1750		
1760	US Population: 1.5M — 65% growth over 20 years	
1760s	Strawbridge, Webb, King come on own	**SYSTEM** — John Wesley determines Wesleyan System/Belief. He broadens the system gradually across UK.
Sept 1764	GW asks Wesley to send preachers	Wesley at his conference determines Arminian doctrine & Methodist structure for UK. Defines UK Methodism within C of E 7 not Dissenter.
1769	**SYSTEM** — Wesley's disciples gather societies into the Wesleyan system — Wesley sends Pilmore & Boardman	
1770	Whitefield dies in America	
1771	Wesley sends Asbury & Wright	
1773	Wesley sends Rankin as his Assistant	
1778	Asbury Remains; Rankin returns; Wesley does not visit America	
1780	US Population: 2.7M — 300% growth over 40 years	England-Wales Population: 7M — 16% growth over 40 years
1781	Battle of Yorktown - American Victory	
1784	**DENOMINATION** with Bishops — **Asbury:** Relational Leadership modifies system — Methodist Episcopal Church: A National system is created separate from Protestant Episcopal Church.	**DENOMINATION** — Wesley Creates his legal hndred — Wesley creates his heir: The Legal Hundred – separate from Church of England.

to them. They walked into spaces known to them from everyday life, such as barns, carriage houses, or under trees. They had their own space in which to meet one another and invite others to join them. Early Methodism was like the 'World Wide Web' (www.) organizes today's internet.

The first missionaries sent by Wesley brought his concept of a connectional system to the colonies. The way his system of connectionalism functioned was based on the idea of a British monarch. It did not take Wesley's 1771 missionary, Francis Asbury, long to understand for Wesley's connectionalism to survive, it must be molded into the new American democratic state after the Revolutionary War. From the time Asbury arrived in Philadelphia until his death in 1816, he devoted his life to the development of American Methodism into a dynamic movement with a special interest in Black people.

The key to Asbury's adaptation was the Quarterly Conference. Quakers had quarterly meetings and John Wesley had quarterly Love Feasts. Asbury transformed the practice of the quarterly meeting into a religious and administrative tool to manage the ministry of a local circuit, usually the size of a county. Asbury structured these four annual meetings into a multi-day, multi-functional event with Love Feasts, evangelistic preaching to the community, and a business meeting that met over a weekend, so Blacks could attend. Throughout the year, two ministers — one senior and the other beginning his ministry - would ride the circuit going from place to place to preach, administer the sacraments of Baptism and Holy Communion, and ensure Methodist order was maintained. It would take several weeks to complete one ride through the circuit. Asbury understood that Americans wanted decisions to be made in a democratic process, unlike Wesley's monarchical decrees, which allowed no voting or any feed-back from his called conference members.

Though chaired by the Presiding Elder, it was the laity of the quarterly conferences who determined who should be a class leader, an exhorter, a local preacher, and expel any member who no longer met Methodist standards, regardless of their race as Black or white Methodists. This mobile structure required many strong leaders at all levels to provide constant oversight of the whole system, in order to train, weed out, and promote capable leaders. That is why the first order of business was to correct or weed out unfit leaders at the quarterly conference level.

As the Methodist membership grew, the system was capable of dividing and reproducing itself. When there were too many Methodists for one Quarterly Conference to manage, a second or third one would be organized in the county. By 1845, Dorchester County (MD) had so many Methodists, it now had three Quarterly Conferences.[98]

With everyone being connected to one another, this connectionalism made Methodism unique in the way other Protestant churches organized themselves. Within the quarterly conference, a new local church could be started within the circuit and remain part of the same quarterly conference. If it separated itself from the others, it was no longer a Methodist church. From the beginning of Methodism to the Civil War, the quarterly conference was the basic unit of interaction and ministry supervision for the Methodist Episcopal Church for Black and white laity.

These quarterly conferences were connected to an annual conference. Above the Annual Conference was the General Conference, which met

---

98 *"General Minutes,"* Methodist Episcopal Church, 1848.

once every four years. The membership of annual and general conferences consisted of only white Traveling Elders and the laity had no voting
rights. A quarterly conference could submit petitions to the annual and
general Conferences for consideration.

A Traveling Elder was a minister who had been approved by
quarterly and annual conferences for ordination to travel wherever the
bishop assigned him for that year. He usually spent two years on a circuit
in a quarterly conference within the same annual conference. After which,
the bishop re-assigned him to another circuit. The whole system was
mobile and met at different places, which allowed for laity to attend the
sessions whenever the meeting was near them.

Asbury ensured all these meetings were democratic. All decisions were
made by majority vote. Although all voting members were white, they
were charged to examine each person, Black and white, for class leader,
exhorter, and local preacher on their spiritual fitness to lead as a Methodist.
This examination was not a pro forma exercise. They removed leaders
and even expelled members from the Methodist society. Before the State
of Maryland changed its manumission laws, the Talbot Quarterly Conference
brought Methodist slaveholders to account to see if they had actually freed
their slaves, instead of buying another slave to take the manumitted one's
place. If they had only replaced a manumitted slave with a purchased
one, that person would be expelled from the Methodist society in Talbot
County.[99]

Though the Methodist Episcopal Church offered many leadership
opportunities to Blacks at the local level, the way the system worked kept
talented Black leaders from 'moving up the ladder' as ordained Traveling

---

99 *Talbot Quarterly Conference Minutes,* 1805-1810.

Elders. They were denied voting rights at Quarterly Conference, Annual Conference, and General Conference. Without having the opportunity to be ordained as a Traveling Elder, there was no possibility of being elected Bishop at General Conference. As African American laity, they could serve as leaders in the ministry but did not hold administrative offices of finance and property, nor vote on quarterly conference decisions. No Black nor white layperson had voting rights at the annual and general conference meetings.

In comparison to the severe restrictions within American society on a Black man's mobility, especially after Nat Turner's Rebellion. A lay Black local preacher could move from one nearby quarterly conference to another to minister, if his credentials were current from his presiding elder and approved by the receiving quarterly conference. At that time, what other organization gave a Black man that kind of status and mobility?

It is easy to focus on the limitations of racism that had on voting rights and legal controls over Black people and overlook the most radical dimension of Methodist ministry: the church organized free and enslaved Africans into groups and gave them their own class leaders and preachers! Sometimes, it had unexpected outcomes, like the leaders of the 1822 Charleston Rebellion were Methodists.

Before the Charleston rebellion, Freeborn Garrettson was whipped nearly to death by a wealthy Centreville (MD) man, John Brown, for his Methodist ministry. Did loud worship cause Mr. Brown to become so angry that he wanted to kill this Methodist Circuit Rider? Could it be that Garrettson and others were organizing Blacks, free and enslaved, into groups? Kill the leader, and the group dissolves? To see Methodism as only about religion is to miss her radical work of creating Black leaders in a society hostile toward their gifts.

The most controversial element of Wesley's connectional system, even to our present time, was the 'Trust Clause.' It was the practice of John Wesley to hold all property, land, and money in collective ownership to ensure the assets were being used for Methodist purposes in his name. In American Methodism, the person of John Wesley was replaced by the annual conference. Each annual conference holds the collective ownership of all Methodist assets. Local trustees managed the property and stewards cared for the money on behalf of the larger American Methodist connection, as long as that church remains a member of the Methodist system. When disputes have arisen and churches have sought to leave, the 'Trust Clause' has become a flashpoint of significant legal disagreements. These struggles began early in American Methodist history with Black Methodism and remain volatile today.

An unexpected benefit from a connectional system was how it helped Harriet Tubman and others in the Underground Railroad in getting slaves to freedom. Methodists had the only church organization that covered the whole Delmarva Peninsula. With annual conference sessions moving every year from place to place, it put clergy supporters of the UGRR in contact with Blacks in that community. Could the Philadelphia Annual Conference meetings in 1845 in Milford, Delaware or 1848 in Easton, Maryland, or 1851 in Smyrna, Delaware, have helped Harriet Tubman and her associates make connections on where her Underground Railroad could travel from the Eastern Shore of Maryland to Wilmington and Philadelphia?

For African Methodists, the American Methodist connectional system gave them physical space, whereby they could experience leadership, personal initiative, and be part of something bigger than themselves—a national church, the nation and God!

America had experienced the thirty-year personal dynamism of George Whitefield, as he preached and set up societies up and down the East Coast and created the infant beginnings of Black societal Methodists. By contrast, Wesley was unknown personally in the colonies; however, his basic connectional system was transformative in creating a system of leadership and spiritual development.

Francis Asbury, through his exceptional leadership, adapted Wesley's connectional system into the American democratic context, which allowed American culture to adopt early Methodism as its largest church. To achieve this spiritual impact, Methodism needed Whitefield, Wesley, and Asbury in that order and in their own time.

Portrait of John Wesley c 1766

by Nathaniel Hone.

CHAPTER 9

African Culture Is Embraced

It is impossible to discern the reason a person chose to become a Methodist. There are observable indicators that made Methodism appealing to African Americans.

Methodists brought with them a program of spiritual change that focused on the person, regardless of race. The preachers were compelled to go to every person because 'God so loved the world.' Another way to express this vision was that because of their race and their conditions in slavery, Methodist preachers reached out with Christian compassion. The slave's life condition was known to them. Some of those preachers, like Garrettson, who had been slave owners, had freed their slaves and became anti-slavery advocates. They consequently pressed other owners to free their slaves, too. That Methodist attitude impressed the enslaved.

The preachers were laity. Their lay status had not been 'educated out' of them, like the Anglican clergy who had been schooled and ordained in London. Their spoken English was the language of the laborer. Their training was riding alongside an experienced preacher to learn how the ministry is practiced and by reading books recommended by the bishop.

These preachers encouraged emotional expressions of shouting, weeping, and enthusiastic singing as a sign of the Spirit's presence. They preached with passion and expected an emotional response. This experience of a divine spirit was understood and sought by Africans from their ancestors. These African religious expressions were brought into worship as they became Methodists. Though Anglican clergy were the first to baptize Africans in America as Christians, their resistance to displays of religious enthusiasm became a barrier for many Blacks.[100] It has been observed: "The black man's worship is older than his church."[101]

In preparation for the 1822 slave revolt in Charleston, South Carolina, Gullah Jack, a Methodist, used his African spirit influence to recruit African-born slaves as soldiers. He provided them with charms as protection and a 'shield' against the whites. In reverse, he used these spiritual powers to terrify others into keeping silent about the conspiracy. These methods helped attract many to join the revolt.

Earlier, George Whitefield wrote in his Journal on Wednesday, January 13, 1740, about traveling at night in South Carolina during the eclipse of the moon.[102] He came across a hut full of Africans with a large fire. Then, a little while later, the moon was shining brightly,

---

100 Anne Polk Diffendal, "The Society for the Propagation of the Gospel in Foreign Parts and the Assimilation of Foreign Protestants in British North America: [Dissertation for University of Nebraska, 1974. P. 13.] "…Anglican missionaries tended to be closer to foreign Protestants who shared their concept of the Church and condemned enthusiasm."

101 Walls, 113.

102 The totality of the eclipse was 104.9 minutes. Peak was at 10:33 p.m. This was a select class of eclipses lasting over 100 minutes.

and in the next hut, they could see Africans dancing around the fire. When they got to the plantation, the master told them of the 'occasion' in which they had been observed.[103] They were clearly engaging in an African ritual brought from their tribe, which the white master knew of and permitted.

John D. Long writes in *Pictures of Slavery in Church and State* about an ecstatic African Prayer Meeting in detail:

> The colored exhorter or leader calls on two or three in succession to pray, filling up the intervals with singing tunes and words composed by themselves. At a given signal of the leader, the men will take off their jackets, hang up their hats, and tie up their heads with handkerchiefs; the women will tighten their turbans; and the company will then form a circle around the singer, and jump and bawl to their heart's content, I have seen colored men, who made no pretensions at all to religion, jump as high as the most devout. After a prolonged continuation of these violent evolutions, some will swoon away; their muscles will become perfectly rigid, and they will lie as motionless as though they were dead. Sand thrown in their eyes, while in this state, will not make them wink. Many persons think this condition is the result of supernatural power, and regard the subjects of it with reverence."[104]

One illustration is seen by Rev. Ridgway, who wrote in his Diary:

> "I preached a TS (tough sermon?) to a crowded house from I Cor 16—22. It was a solemn time. After the congregation had gone *the blacks in the yard broke out in a shout.* The whites returned to

---

103 Whitefield, George, *"Journals"* (Grand Rapids: Christian Classics reprint, 2000), page 247. It incorrectly gives date January 2 which is a Saturday.

104 John D. Long, *Pictures of Slavery in Church and State*, [1857], p 356.

see what was the matter. Several seem cut to the heart. I hope they won't soon forget it."[105] [July 4, 1805] *(Emphasis added)*

A *New York Times* reporter wrote about a 2016 discovery on the Lloyd Plantation in Queen Anne's County, Maryland, where Frederick Douglass and his mother had been slaves:

In the late 18th century, Methodist Episcopal (Church) . . . preachers carried the Christian message to the plantations on Maryland's Eastern Shore. They seemed to have been successful converting slaves, in part by giving new meaning to traditional symbols. For example, a powerful symbol from the BaKongo belief system in West Central Africa, where many of the slaves came from, was the cosmogram, a circle with an X inside.

African Americans repurposed these materials because they had symbolic value as well in the form of Ezekiel's blazing chariot wheel, Dr. Pruitt said.

The wheel imagery is described in the Book of Ezekiel 10:9-10:

And when I looked, behold the four wheels by the cherubim, one wheel by one cherub, and another wheel by another cherub and the appearance of the wheels was as the color of aberyl stone. And as for their appearances, the four had one likeness, as if a wheel had been in the midst of a wheel.

The wheel-like image in the Book of Ezekiel and the cosmogram, Dr. Elizabeth Pruitt suggested,

represented the universe, and the path we travel through this world and the afterlife," and "it stands for the enduring connections between this world and the next, the power from above and below.

---

105   James Ridgway, *Diary*, Unpublished. July 4, 1805.

For the first time, the two circle images had been found together virtually side by side. It seems that the Christian preachers had discovered the powerful resonance the wheel image held for African Americans. One of the most popular spirituals among people in . . . (the) churches and camp meetings on the Eastern Shore is "'Zekiel Saw the Wheel."

'Zekiel saw de wheel, way up in the middle of the air
'Zekiel saw de wheel, way up in the middle of the air
De big wheel run by faith, little wheel by the grace of God
Wheel in a wheel, way in de middle of de air.'

An African-Methodist Episcopal bishop in the 19th century, Daniel Payne, wrote that the circle and wheel imagery extended the "Ring Shout," in which participants move counterclockwise, singing and dancing at camp meetings. This motion is in the same direction as the cycle of life in the cosmogram. It was said that "sinners won't get converted unless there is a ring here, a ring there, a ring over yonder, or sinners will not get converted."[106]

Here are key conditions that possibly influenced Africans to become Methodists:

1. Africans were welcomed and respected.

2. The African style of worship was affirmed.

3. Meetings took place outside of a church building.

4. Africans—enslaved and free—had the opportunities for status: class leaders, certified as Exhorters and Local Preachers, earned tickets for Love Feasts and participated in camp meetings and quarterly conferences.

---

106 John Noble Wilford, *New York Times,* November 7, 2016 "Ezekiel's Wheel Ties African Spiritual Traditions to Christianity." *Used by Permission.*

5. In the early days, class meetings were interracial and later, African Americans had their own groups by choice within the Methodist Church's Quarterly Conferences (Segregation came after the Civil War).

6. For many Methodist leaders slavery was discouraged and some Methodist slave owners had freed their slaves.

CHAPTER 10

Asbury Ordains Africans

African American Methodists knew of Francis Asbury's notable support for their ministry. Coming from England, he got to know Black people personally as slaves, and freedmen and freedwomen. For him African Americans were present and always 'seen.' They were not 'wallpaper' only to be noticed when something happened in white society that involved them. He was an unusual white man - a British citizen who became a friend of the African people.

His awareness of their lives enabled him to choose Black Harry Hosier as his traveling associate. The esteem Asbury had for Harry's preaching ability allowed him to preach to both Africans and whites. Everyone who had heard both men speak agreed that Harry was the better preacher! This allowed Africans who were uneducated like Harry to freely associate with Asbury.[107]

They also saw Asbury use his position to support Richard Allen during his years-long conflict with the white clergy in Philadelphia. As

---

107 Harry also rode with Bishop Coke who praised him in his *Journal* (1793), page 18. Quoted by Frederick A. Norwood, *The Story of American Methodism* (Nashville: Abingdon Press, 1974), p. 168.

a lay local preacher, Allen was under the authority of the Philadelphia Quarterly Conference, which could at any time remove his license for ministry. By ordaining Allen, Asbury removed him from direct authority of the Quarterly Conference, which made him responsible to Bishop Asbury for his ministerial credentials. At that time, ordinations were done under the name of the bishop and not the annual conference. Asbury further showed his support by ordaining Allen as a deacon one year before the General Conference provided legislation for the deacon ordination of African Americans.

The whole church witnessed Asbury's dedication to African Americans with his ordinations of other talented and committed African Americans who were serving as lay local preachers. All those early Black Methodist clergy, who later formed independent Black Methodist denominations, had Asbury's fingerprints on their heads. The only exception was Peter Spencer.[108]

The rightly celebrated Absalom Jones became the first Black man ordained Deacon in the Protestant Episcopal Church in 1795. Though Jones was the first Black American to receive Christian ordination and to be ordained a Priest in 1804, it would be another twenty-two years (1826) before another Black Episcopal clergyman would be ordained in Philadelphia. The first Black Philadelphia Presbyterian pastor to be ordained was John Gloucester on April 13, 1810.[109]

---

108 Coker, Daniel, *A Dialogue Between a Virginian and African Minister* (1810) quoted in *Pamphlets of Protest*, p. 64.

109 Historical Society of Pennsylvania Webpage, '*The Church Awakens: African Americans and the Struggle for Justice*,' Leadership Gallery: The Reverend Peter Williams, Jr. ["Williams was ordained a deacon in 1820 and a priest in 1826. He was the second African American to be ordained a priest in The Episcopal Church following Absalom Jones whose ordination had occurred in the Diocese of Pennsylvania in 1804."] and *Historical Society of Pennsylvania Webpage, Reverend John Gloucester: 'Former Slave Turned Presbyterian Minister'.*

Once Asbury ordained the second Black American, Richard Allen, not long after the ordination of Absolom Jones, he set about ordaining Black leaders from Baltimore to New York City. His ordinations created the leadership foundation for Black Methodism that exists today in America.

Bishop Francis Asbury

Figure 3: List of known Methodist Episcopal Black Ordinations.

DATE		LOCATION	BISHOP
June 11, 1799	Richard Allen	Philadelphia	Asbury
May 16, 1806	James Varick[110]	John Street New York City	Asbury
May 16, 1806	Abraham Thompson	John Street New York City	Asbury
May 16, 1806	June Scott	John Street New York City	Asbury
April 27, 1808	Daniel Coker[111]	Zion Church, New York City	Asbury
April 27, 1808	William Miller	Zion Church, New York City	Asbury
1809	John Charleston	Virginia	McKendree
April 9, 1809	Jacob Tapisco	Zoar Church, Philadelphia	Asbury
	James Champion[112]	Zoar Church, Philadelphia	Asbury
Before 1810	Jeffrey Buley	Philadelphia	Asbury
1812	The General Conference made Local Deacons eligible for Elders' Orders		
May 15, 1815	George White[113]	New York City	Asbury
Unknown	Unknown former slave in the South		Asbury

---

110   Asbury Journal 2, page 506.
111   Ibid, page 568.
112   Wayman, *Cyclopedia of African Methodism*, page 34.
113   Walls, page 52.

The record of Methodists ordaining African men is truly remarkable in comparison to other churches and the attitudes in the larger society. In fifteen years, Bishop Asbury ordained Allen, four Black men in Philadelphia, six in New York, and an unknown former slave. In the meantime, Bishop William McKendree ordained one Black man in Virginia. By 1816, two Methodist bishops had ordained a total of twelve known African Americans.

When the African Methodist Episcopal Church (AME) was organized as a new denomination in 1816, the consecration of Richard Allen as bishop made him the first African American bishop in the United States.[114] Those who laid their hands upon him were most likely Rev. Daniel Coker, Rev. Jacob Tapsco, Rev. James Champion, and Rev. Jeremiah Bulah, who had all been ordained by Bishop Asbury. The fifth person in Allen's consecration was his old friend, the Episcopalian priest, Rev. Absalom Jones.

An interesting aside is the story of the Rev. William Miller. Raised in Centreville, Maryland, in the Methodist Episcopal Church, he became an African Methodist Episcopal colleague with Richard Allen in Philadelphia. Later, he became the third bishop of the African Methodist Episcopal Zion Church. He had been a member of all three Methodist denominations that had Black clergy.[115]

Asbury's ordination of an unknown slave is intriguing to speculate on who and where it happened. Could it have taken place in Charleston,

114 It was 104 years later before the successor of MEC, The Methodist Church, consecrated Black Bishops Robert E. Jones and Matthew W. Clair, Sr. in 1920. Thomas, page 175.

115 Walls, William J., *The African Methodist Episcopal Zion Church: Reality of the Black Church* (A.M.E. Zion Publishing House, 1974), page 567.

South Carolina, with its large African-American Methodist constituency? He started his yearly visitations up the East Coast from Charleston, South Carolina. Very easily, he could have ordained a leader, as he did in Philadelphia and New York. The reason Asbury may not have recorded his name was to minimize the danger such a radical act would have placed upon him and other Black preachers in the South.

Bishop Asbury's impact in seeking out and ordaining African-American Methodists is extraordinary. The exact number will never be known. What is known is that no one invested more of himself in identifying African American Methodist leaders than Francis Asbury.

By 1821, all of these ordained Black clergy had left the Methodist Episcopal Church for leadership roles in the African Methodist Episcopal Church and African Methodist Episcopal Zion Church. Asbury's leadership role is indisputable in providing the ordained clergy for these two new denominations. Each ordained person who left was not re-ordained. They understood the profound significance of their ordination by Asbury.

CHAPTER 11

Asbury Shapes The Development of African Methodism

With the growth of Methodism, Asbury recognized by 1806 that African Methodism in the Baltimore-Philadelphia-New York corridor needed its own clergy leaders, so he proceeded methodically to ordain Black clergy. The question is: 'Why did Asbury ordain them?' Ordination is for sacramental ministry. Black members had access to the sacraments through the white clergy in their Quarterly Conferences. Though it did ensure a sacramental ministry would be available long-term to Blacks, regardless of white clergy attitudes, it was not for the lack of current access to the sacramentals. The answer is in the second question: 'Why did Bishop Asbury ordain African leaders at this time?'

The answer rests in Asbury's knowledge of America that he expressed in his Journal entry on February 1, 1809, after an exhausting conference in Virginia:

"We are defrauded of great numbers by the pains that are taken to keep the blacks from us; their masters are afraid of the influence of our principles. Would not an amelioration in the condition and treatment of the slaves have produced more practical good to the poor Africans than any attempt at their emancipation? The state of society, unhappily, does not admit of this: besides, the blacks are deprived of the means of instruction; who will take the pains to lead them into the way of salvation, and watch over them that they may not stray, but the Methodists?"[116]

No one in America had the pulse of the average person more than Asbury. The longer he traveled up and down the American coastline of the thirteen colonies, he came to believe that slavery would not end with voluntary manumissions by enslavers, especially in the South. Thomas Jefferson was ending his presidency, and James Madison was to assume the office within weeks. He had met all the early presidents. Though George Washington, who shortly after meeting with Asbury, had provided manumission for his slaves, Asbury knew that Jefferson and Madison were slave holders. He knew that with 1808 coming, they were not interested in freeing their slaves. Like he did with Washington, he no doubt raised the issue during his visits, after which they took the oath of office.

The timing is significant as it relates to the United States Constitution, Article 1. Section 9. Clause 1, which eliminated the importation of slaves in 1808. Jefferson, in his annual message to Congress in December 1806, noted the approaching deadline. Congress passed a statute prohibiting the importation, effective January 1, 1808. To a person like Asbury, its effect meant the existing status of slaves gave little hope of

---

116   Asbury, *Journal II*, page 591.

freedom. Their value increased as an essential member of the labor force. No owner would be inclined to manumit a slave whose value was increasing and the uncertainty about the supply of new workers. This must have weighed heavily on Asbury's mind, as he contemplated how he should respond to this change. By the time he met the Virginians one year later, he could see a bleak future for the enslaved African Americans.

For those today who believe Asbury had lessened his commitment to freeing the slaves must consider the conditions of his time. The time had expired on convincing enslavers of their moral duty to free their enslaved labor. Asbury saw clearly that there was to be no immediate end to slavery. No one could have predicted slavery's end, even in 1860. Slavery's defeat came fifty-six years after Asbury's Virginia comments, but not through manumission. It came with Union war victories. In July 1863 Lee was defeated at Gettysburg and Grant captured at Vicksburg. This gave the opportunity for Abraham Lincoln to be re-elected in 1864. It took the determined waging of the American Civil War to last four long violent and bloody years to crush southern slave society to end slavery. It was not ended by the passionate words of the abolition movement nor by the Methodist General Conference resolutions or Asbury's efforts at manumission.

With his failing health Asbury knew he did not have the time left nor the physical strength to continue as vigorously as he had earlier in his ministry. His health had declined so severely in his last two years that he had to be carried like a child by his assistant, John Wesley Bond. With what strength he had for these last seven years, he focused the authority of his office to ensure the future of African American Methodism would survive him.

Asbury knew the Africans had the abilities and talents to lead themselves forward in spite of their constricted reality. As his ability to stand and walk declined, he ordained New York Deacons between 1806 and 1808 and in Philadelphia 1808-1809 (Allen 1799). As bishop, he did not need the General or Annual Conferences to empower a new generation of African Methodist leadership. He could do it himself.

Even before he ordained Black clergy, he supported the building of African churches in Philadelphia (1794), Baltimore (1795), and New York (1796). This provided for African Methodist identities within their city's quarterly conferences.[117] Within these ministries, the future clergy were formed and identified for ordination. In response to his labors on their behalf, Black fathers named their sons after the man who had no sons. In 1813, the first church to be named Asbury was established in New York City. Others did the same in Baltimore and Washington, DC.

Though most Black Methodists lived in the South, he understood

---

117 Asbury in his *Journal*, May 30, 1795, while in Maryland, wrote: "I met the Africans, to consult about building a house, and forming a distinct African, yet Methodist Church." Two years later, June 25, 1797, while in Baltimore, he pursued his intent of organizing the African Americans: "I obtained the liberty of the managers of the African academy [school for black children] to congregate the fathers as well as to teach the children. We had nearly five hundred coloured people ... I am trying to organize the African church." The origins of Sharp Street Memorial Methodist Church, Baltimore. According to his Journal, Asbury was in New York in September as well. Asbury, Vol III Letters February 11, 1797, p.160: "the Africans (New York) are about building one; help them all you (Rev George Roberts) can. The more houses the more people; the more preachers, and the more converted." In 1813 a second African Chapel was founded and took the name "Asbury."

On June 29, 1794, Bishop Asbury opened the African Church, called Bethel, in Philadelphia.

that the course he had started in the urban north was unworkable in the South. Throughout Methodism in rural North, southern African Methodism in the Methodist Episcopal Church would continue to function as it had since its inception, with the quarterly conference being the basic organization of ministry with its classes, exhorters, and local Black preachers.

Asbury used the last decade of his life to ensure northern urban African Methodism was sustainable beyond him. He began an expression of Methodism, whereby her members could shape the future themselves. Asbury was committed to the Methodist Episcopal Church. It has to be asked: Did he, deep within his heart, realize he was preparing for the time when most Black Methodists would no longer be part of his denomination?

This land, which we have watered with our tears and our blood, is now our mother country, and we are well satisfied to stay where wisdom abounds and the gospel is free.

Bishop Richard Allen's Letter to *Freedom's Journal*, November 2, 1827, page 134.

CHAPTER 12

Richard Allen: Slave to Bishop

The most famous African American was Richard Allen, who was born a slave to Benjamin Chew and lived north of Dover, Delaware. Allen was sold by Chew to his neighbor, Stokely Sturgis. Described by Allen as a kind and good man, he fell on hard times and sold Allen's mother to another slave master to remain financially solvent. This broke up Allen's family.

Allen's Methodism began before he was sold to Sturgis. Since he remained in the area, Allen continued to actively participate in the weekly class meetings. Since these weekly meetings did not require a church building, they gathered on the property of Benjamin Wells and were led by John Gray.

As devout Methodists, Allen and his brother resolved to demonstrate their commitment to hard work and were willing to miss class meetings and preaching services to ensure their day's work was completed. It was important to Allen that the man who held him in bondage witness the genuineness of his Methodist faith. More importantly, Allen desired Sturgis's Christian conversion.

Over time, Allen persuaded Sturgis to allow Methodists to hold services at his house. That brought Freeborn Garrettson to preach to his master on Daniel 5:27 – *"Thou art weighed in the balance, and art found wanting."* Garrettson used many examples of people being weighed in the balance, but the worst were the slaveholders. He spoke with the authority as a former slaveholder who freed his slaves upon converting to Methodism.

Garrettson's message was so compelling that Sturgis believed himself to be one of those "wanting" before God's Day of Judgment. Sturgis sought to correct his error by offering Allen and his brother the opportunity to buy their freedom for sixty pounds in gold or silver or two thousand dollars of Continental money.[118] For fear that Sturgis might experience economic instability again, the two brothers continued to work hard to gain their freedom quickly.

In his manumission paper, Allen was known as Negro Richard. Upon gaining his freedom in August 1783, he took the surname Allen. He does not give his reason for this choice, but perhaps he was aligning himself with William Allen, a well-known Pennsylvania jurist who had been Benjamin Chew's neighbor.[119]

After a period of ministry in the mid-Atlantic states, Allen brought his drive to build a viable African American Methodist presence to the city of brotherly love. Allen embraced all the possibilities of Philadelphia, as an ambitious young man wanting to make his mark on the world. The Revolutionary victory over the British filled the air with the excitement of building a new nation. He took his place

---

118 Richard S. Newman, *Freedom's Prophet: Bishop Richard Allen, the AME Church, and the Black Founding Fathers* (New York, New York: University Press, 2008), pages 43-44.

119 Ibid, 45.

among those seeking to prosper financially and spiritually. The spiritual center of Methodism was St. George's Church. There, he joined in with other Black and white Americans in class meetings and worship services.

Like the city, St. George's was undergoing the strain of growth and change. The common folk liked the traditional enthusiastic Methodist worship, while the prosperous members preferred a more ordered service. Within this mix were the African Americans, whose numbers were rapidly increasing. Unfortunately, this promising environment became a combustible mix of misunderstandings and fractured relationships. For example, in 1801, fifty white members left St. George's to start the United Society of People Called Methodist (later called Union M.E. Church). They met in the building Benjamin Franklin had built in 1740 to accommodate those flocking to hear the dynamic preaching of British evangelist George Whitefield.[120]

Meanwhile, Black members had been accustomed to sitting among whites in the sanctuary as a sign of equality in the house of God. White leaders initiated changes in seating, and the Black worshippers were moved to seats along the back wall. Renovations were undertaken to address the overcrowding problem. Like good members, Allen and other Black members made financial contributions in support of the effort. When they returned to the church, they discovered to their dismay that their seats had been moved to the balcony.

It is unclear whether it was at this service or a subsequent one when a very unfortunate incident occurred at the communion rail. Though the exact date is unknown, the consequences have never been forgotten. As Black members knelt in prayer at the communion

120 www.havertownumc.org. History of our Church.

rail, a white usher asked them to get up. Allen asked to be left alone until they had finished. The usher insisted and took Allen by the arm and pulled him to his feet. The insulting gesture prompted Allen, Absalom Jones, and others to begin securing their own worship space.

Before the incident Allen and Absalom Jones worked together in creating the Free African Society, a mutual aid society for free Africans. Over time the members of the society would become St. Thomas Episcopal Church and Allen sought his own leadership within the Philadelphia Methodist Circuit.[121]

With his incredible drive Allen raised the funds to build Bethel Church.[122] He wanted the property under his control while remaining in the Philadelphia Methodist Circuit. This was the arrangement Absalom Jones had with the leaders of the Philadelphia Episcopal Church in developing St. Thomas Episcopal Church. Unlike Allen, Jones had had a long relationship with the Christ - St. Peter's vestry and his former enslaver was a member of the vestry with whom he still worked with in the business. For Allen who did not have the same relational ties, this put him into direct conflict with a long-held Methodist practice, the Trust Clause, which means all local church assets are held "in trust for the benefit of the entire denomination." The Trust Clause was instituted by Methodism's founder, John Wesley, who required all Methodist properties to be deeded in his name. That gave him the power to ensure the preacher and the Methodist

---

121 John Wigger, *American Saint: Francis Asbury and The Methodists* (Oxford: Oxford University Press, 2009), pages 247-252.

122 Asbury Journal, February 14, 1797, records the Africans will donate 100 pounds to rebuilding Bethel in Charleston, SC. After the Civil War MEC (North) gained control of the building and it was moved and became what is known today as Old Bethel UMC. At least two Black John Street members donated toward its building. Where possible, Africans contributed to the building of the first churches.

society abided by Wesleyan doctrine and practices If they disobeyed him, he removed the preacher and closed the society. In America, that practice moved from the person of Wesley to the Annual Conference. In Allen's situation, it was the Philadelphia Annual Conference. A property could not be deeded outside the Methodist Episcopal Church and remain Methodist.

When Allen approached the Presiding Elder with his plan for deeding the Bethel property outside the conference, he assumed the Presiding Elder had agreed with him. The Presiding Elder said he would take care of the incorporation articles, but he did it contrary to Allen's intention. The Elder had Bethel incorporated in the name of the Philadelphia Conference.

A few years later, Allen discovered the betrayal and applied the full force of his will to remove the Conference Trust Clause from the deed and its incorporation. To rectify his legal quandary within the church, he needed to convince the Philadelphia Annual Conference of his position by a two-thirds vote. No Methodist Episcopal governing body has been inclined to make an exception to this rule, even today.

Allen's indomitable will and the conference's solid resistance clashed against each other. The struggle brought threats to have Allen thrown out of the Methodist Episcopal connection for disobeying the discipline of the church. The conflict continued until early 1816. Allen went outside the church to the Pennsylvania Supreme Court. The court granted Allen his long desire to have Bethel Church deeded to him without the Methodist Trust Clause. The Trust Clause did not have the legal status within the Commonwealth of Pennsylvania as it did within the Methodist conference.

The Trust Clause conflict would have been intense regardless of Allen's race. The conflict would have caused a lesser man to give up and leave the Methodist Church. Although the insult to his dignity as a free Black man would have been insufferable, through it all, he remained a member of the Methodist Episcopal Church until 1816, when he and others left to form the African Methodist Episcopal Church.

Allen and Asbury

Throughout Allen's ministry, Bishop Francis Asbury was his constant ally. Allen met Asbury for the first time when he was still enslaved on Stokely Sturgis's farm, which was located at a crossroads where Methodist circuit riders frequently passed through looking for occasions to preach. Asbury arrived on Friday, August 13, 1779, at Benjamin Wells' forest. He preached on the Book of Revelation 22:11—15 and met with Allen's class. Asbury described the encounter as "affectionate."[123]

Richard Allen was the kind of Methodist Asbury who was looking to enlist in leadership. The two men met again the next year in Baltimore under very different circumstances. Allen was now a free man and a preaching Methodist. Asbury was now one of two Methodist Episcopal bishops.

Richard Whatcoat, later a bishop, observed Allen's abilities firsthand and knew Asbury needed a traveling partner to help him preach to Africans and whites. Asbury believed he had found a worthy companion in Allen. But once Allen heard about the conditions Asbury sought when riding through the South, he bristled at the offer. Feeling that traveling South made him vulnerable to harm, he refused the offer. Allen's objection did not change Asbury's esteem for the man, nor Allen's for Asbury.[124]

---

123 Francis Asbury, *Journals*, August 13, 1779.
124 Wigger, 244-246

Not long afterward, Allen moved to Philadelphia and joined a class at St. George's in February 1786. Until the end of Asbury's life, the two men were in regular contact. It has been observed that the two of them formed "a great interracial friendship, a very uncommon thing in later eighteenth-century America."[125]

During the conflict over the status of Bethel Church, Asbury supported Allen by his presence and authority as bishop. After Bethel was built, Asbury preached the dedicatory sermon for all to see; he wanted Allen in the Methodist Episcopal Church. At the most intense periods of Allen's conflict in Philadelphia with the Methodist leadership, Asbury used his behind-the-scenes problem-solving skills and called on his dear friends, Ezekiel Cooper and Freeborn Garrettson, to serve as Presiding Elders. Both had known Allen well for many years. Mutual trust between them gave Allen the support he needed to keep him within the Methodist Episcopal Church.

It is commonly understood that Asbury had softened his later support of Allen by refraining from ordaining him an Elder. Is it true that he did not ordain him Elder? It is well established that Richard Allen was ordained Deacon by Bishop Asbury on June 11, 1799, one year before the General Conference formally approved such an ordination. It is intriguing to think that this was Asbury's way of pushing the General Conference to action for the sake of his African-American members. No one was putting pressure on Asbury to act before the General Conference. His actions sprang from within himself.[126]

---

125 Richard S. Newman, page 48.

126 John Wigger, American Saint, page 491, note 15. Absalom Jones was ordained in the Protestant Episcopal Church as a Deacon in 1795 and Priest in 1804, specifically to serve as rector of St. Thomas's African Church; however, St. Thomas Church was not admitted to the annual Episcopal convention until 1862.

What if Asbury sought to protect him and elevate his status by ordaining him an Elder to protect him from the ongoing conflicts within the Philadelphia Quarterly Conference? The answer is not in Asbury's Journal, because he seldom recorded anyone's ordination.[127] The primary source that specifically mentions Allen's Elder status before 1816 is *The History of the Methodist Episcopal Church (1845)*[128] by Nathan Bangs:

> ". . . with Richard Allen, a colored local preacher – an elder in the Methodist Episcopal Church—at their head."[129]

> "... since he had exercised the office of a preacher and an elder, obtained great influence over his brethren in the Church."[130]

In Bangs' record of the formation of the African Methodist Episcopal Church, we may assume he had been previously ordained Elder by Asbury. There is no record of him needing to be ordained Elder by the new AMEC. As Wigger writes of Allen's election and consecration to the office of bishop in the African Methodist Episcopal Church, he includes the status of the five local elders who consecrated him:

> "Richard Allen was elected to the office of a bishop, and was consecrated by prayer and the imposition of the hands of five colored local elders, one of whom, Absalom Jones, was a priest of the Protestant Episcopal Church."[131]

---

127 John Wigger, *American Saint*, page, 294. Asbury ordained at least twelve others as deacons, including James Varick (New York) and Daniel Coker (Baltimore).
Asbury noted: "A charge has been brought against me for ordaining a slave, but there was no further pursuit of the case when it was discovered that I was ready with my certificates to prove his freedom." James A. Handy, *Scraps of AME History* refers to the 1799 ordination on page 25.

128 Nathan Bangs, *History of Methodist Episcopal Church* (1845) May 2, 1778 – May 3, 1862) was almost 39 when Asbury died and Allen left MEC. Shortly afterward, he was in charge of the Book Concern in Philadelphia. J. M. Buckley, *American Church History Series: A History of the Methodists* (1896) also notes of Allen's Elder ordination but he may have been quoting Bangs.

129 Ibid, page 30.

130 Ibid, page 32.

131 Ibid, page 32.

Another secondary source is James A. Handy's *Scraps of AME History* (1902). Handy does not mention Bishop Allen's ordination, or the need for him to be ordained, as an Elder during the first session of the General Convention to form an Ecclesiastical Compact where he was elected and consecrated as a bishop.[132] This confirms what Bangs had written about Allen being an Elder while a members of the Methodist Episcopal Church.

African American Methodists followed to the letter the historical Methodist precedent for ordination: Deacon, Elder, and Bishop. One of the first actions taken by the African Methodist Episcopal Zion Church was to ordain James Varick as an Elder before he was elected Bishop.[133] To be a Bishop, he was required to be an Elder first. As noted earlier, Varick had been ordained a Deacon by Asbury.

Many years later, in 1870 the Colored Methodist Episcopal Church followed the traditional Methodist order of Deacon, Elder, Bishop in electing William Henry Miles and Richard H. Vanderhorst to the office of Bishop.[134]

How did Bishop Asbury understand his authority as a bishop to ordain African-American Methodists, like Richard Allen? Early Methodists strove to follow the practices established by John Wesley. We

---

132 James A. Handy, *Scraps of AME History*, Chapter 3, 32ff and 40. Unfortunately, the minutes of the meeting were not preserved and were recreated one-year later by those who were present.

133 William J. Walls, *The African Methodist Episcopal Zion Church: Reality of the Black Church*, 1974. 83.

134 Othal Hawthorne Lakey, *History of the CME Church*, Chapter 7, 189-223. As an aside, note how traditional these first independent Black denominations named themselves: African Methodist Episcopal Church, African Methodist Episcopal Zion Church, Colored Methodist Episcopal Church. Most African American Methodists remained in the Methodist Episcopal Church. It may be of interest to note that Peter Spencer named his church Union Church of Africans. He followed some distinctives of Methodist Episcopal Church and discarded others, like control of church property and selecting your own pastor. He was not ordained by Asbury, nor did he seem to enjoy a close relationship with him. This may be reflected in the way he named and organized his new church in 1813.

can readily see Asbury acting, as John Wesley did, when he ordained Richard Whatcoat and others for service in America in 1784. Without an election by a church body, Wesley and Asbury believed each had the authority by their office to ordain those deemed eligible.[135]

Wesley continued the practice of ordaining people in 1789 when he ordained Thomas Rankin, after he had returned from his ministry in America.[136] This example illustrates that Wesley understood himself as having that authority within himself and not as a one-time emergency response to the American need for an ordained clergy, when the Anglican Bishop of London refused to ordain Methodists for America.

Another example is Thomas Coke, whom Wesley made General Superintendent, who later took the title of bishop. He ordained Asbury in 1784 in Baltimore and James Alexander in 1794, three

---

135   The 1812 Discipline, Chapter 1 Section 1, page 5—7:

"...requested the late Rev. John Wesley to take such measures, in his wisdom and prudence, as would afford them suitable relief in their distress.

In consequence of this, our venerable friend, who under God, had been the Father of the great revival of religion now extending over the earth, by the means of the Methodists, determined to ordain ministers for America; and for this purpose, in the year 1784, sent over three regularly ordained clergy: but preferring the Episcopal mode of church government to any other, he solemnly set apart, by the imposition of his hands, and prayer, one of them, viz. Thomas Coke, Doctor of Civil Law, late of Jesus—college, the University of Oxford, and a Presbyter of the Church of England, for the episcopal office; and having delivered to him letters of episcopal orders, commissioned and directed him to set apart Francis Asbury, then general assistant of the Methodist society in America, for the same episcopal office, he, the said Francis Asbury being first ordained deacon and elder. In consequence of which, the said Francis Asbury was solemnly set apart for the said episcopal office, by prayer, and the imposition of the hands of the said Thomas Coke, other regularly ordained ministers assisting in the sacred ceremony. At which time the General Conference. Held at Baltimore, did unanimously receive the said Thomas Coke and Francis Asbury as their bishops, being fully satisfied of the validity of their episcopal ordination."

136   John Wesley died in 1791.

years after Wesley died in England.[137] In his handwritten ordination certificate, Coke refers to the Church as the Methodist Episcopal Church, of which he was bishop. Here is an Anglican priest, elected as an American Methodist bishop, ordaining a British Methodist in England beyond the bounds of the American Church after Wesley's death!

Asbury was well-versed in the Philadelphia situation involving Bethel Church and Richard Allen's ministry. He had taken the action of appointing presiding elders over the Methodist work who better understood Allen and were supportive of his mission to relieve some of the pressure on him.[138] With Asbury in Philadelphia in April 1815 and close by in June 1815, he could have ordained Allen as a way of showing his support for his ministry, because the Discipline allowed bishops to ordain clergy at their convenience with other elders present.[139] By ordaining Allen, an Elder, Asbury pushed the limits of African American ordination beyond what was thought possible in the Methodist Episcopal Church and the United States of America.

---

137 James Alexander's Ordination Certificate, Wesley Chapel Museum, London, England. 'These are to certify, that I, Thomas Coke, Bishop of the Methodist Episcopal Church, did on this day, in the fear of God and with a single eye to his glory, by the imposition of my hands and prayer, set apart James Alexander for the office of an Elder in the Church of God, believing him to be duly qualified for that said office and I do accordingly recommend him as a proper person to feed the Church of God and administer the holy Sacraments. Given by my hand and seal the 15th day of April, in the year 1794.' Original in Wesley Chapel Museum, London.

138 Wigger, 250. Asbury asked Freeborn Garrettson to be Presiding Elder who had convinced Richard Allen's owner to free his slaves and Ezekiel Cooper who was very supportive of Allen.

139 *1812 Discipline.* Section XX. OF THE LOCAL PREACHERS.

"A local deacon shall be eligible to the office of an elder, after he has preached for four years from the time he was ordained a deacon, and has obtained a recommendation from two thirds of the quarterly meeting conference of which he is a member, certifying his qualifications ... the whole being examined by the annual conference, and if approved, he may be ordained; provided, nevertheless, no slave holder shall be eligible to the office of an elder, where the laws will admit of emancipation, and permit the liberated slave to enjoy freedom."

For forty-six years, Allen and Asbury had remained very close and were an unlikely couple. One was a former Englishman; the other a former slave. Bishop Asbury received little compensation for his tireless efforts; Allen became financially comfortable. On one occasion, Allen bought Asbury a horse because he knew he needed one. Asbury died with only his personal belongings, while Allen left an estate.

When Asbury was near death, Allen took the decisive step to leave the Methodist Episcopal Church and take his beloved Bethel Church with him. Unlike Peter Spencer who took little from the Methodist Episcopal Church when he started his denomination, Richard Allen and his colleagues brought seven gifts into the formation of the African Methodist Episcopal Church from the Methodist Episcopal Church:

1. His conversion to Christianity.

2. His freedom was achieved through the preaching of Freeborn Garrettson, who convinced Stokley Sturgis, his owner, to free him.

3. His friendship with Francis Asbury, who supported him until his own death.

4. His ordination for ministry by Bishop Francis Asbury.

5. His four colleagues were ordained by Bishop Asbury, who in turned consecrated Allen as bishop.

6. African members from St. George's Church who knew how to administer classes (small groups)

7. Replicating the spiritual formation system of the Methodist Episcopal Church.

CHAPTER 13

African-Americans Decide Their Future: Separation

The tensions over how the mother Methodist Episcopal Church was to be governed and how she was to fulfill the aspirations of her Black Methodists pulled the church apart. Cracks first appeared in 1792 when James O'Kelley formed the Republican Methodist Church in reaction to the power of a bishop. That set the stage for Peter Spencer to build the first democratic version of African Methodism within the larger American Methodism.

Peter Spencer, living in Wilmington, Delaware, was an innovative African American leader. He bristled against the control of the Asbury Methodist Episcopal Church's white trustees over Ezion Methodist Episcopal Church. Heated exchanges over several years between Spencer and the trustees were so intense much later someone was so embarrassed by the arguments that they cut out the pages from the trustee and quarterly conference minutes.[140] However, this June 19, 1805, entry remains in the Trustee Minutes:

---

140 Ashbury Records at Barratt's Chapel, Frederica, Delaware.

"Whereas in consequence of meeting the classes of the Black people on the lower seats of this Church, a number of the benches have been broken, and the house, so defiled by dirt, etc., as to render it unfit to meet in, and if any longer tolerate more injury may be sustained (sic) --

Resolved that no Black class shall hereafter meet on the lower floor of Asbury Church, and if they refuse to meet in the gallery, the sexton was to inform them that the door will not be opened for their reception – And furthermore, the leaders of the same are requested to respect this resolution and govern themselves accordingly."[141]

This may be the date Ezion established her own meeting place within the Asbury Quarterly Conference.

This was also a time when Asbury Church was placed in a larger circuit.[142] This meant instead of a resident pastor assigned to Asbury, he had to cover a much larger area. With the loss of a resident pastor, it appears communication became infrequent and stress accelerated, especially between the 100+ white members and 98+ Black members. The church leadership petitioned Bishop Asbury to have Asbury removed from the circuit and their station status restored.[143]

Once a resident preacher was restored to Asbury, its Black membership increased slightly over the whites: 1811-137 Black (white 137) members; 1812-178 Black (white 142) members; 1813-46 Black (white 138) members; and 1814-71 Black (white 123) members.[144] The story is told of Peter Spencer having trouble with the assigned minister. That minister appears to be George Sheets, who left Asbury in 1814 and quit the ministry two years later.[145] He may not have had the best skills in dealing with people.

---

141   Ibid.

142   *General Minutes of Methodist Episcopal Church, 1804-1806.*

143   *Letter March 15, 1808* at Barratt's Chapel.

144   *Asbury Methodist Church Records, 1789-1834.*

145   E.C. Hallman, *Garden of Methodism,* page 84.

Wilmington Black Separation

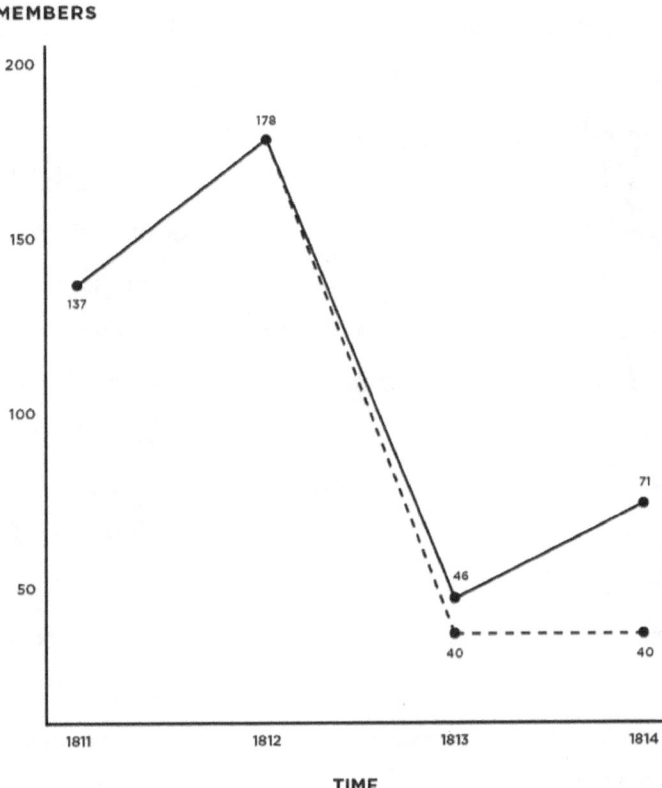

MEMBERS

TIME

Ezion: ────────────────────

Spencer: ─ ─ ─ ─ ─ ─ ─ ─ ─ ─ ─ ─ ─ ─ ─ ─ ─ ─ ─

Source: General Minutes, Methodist Episcopal Church, 1811-1814

With his forty people, probably his class at Ezion, Spencer created the Union Church of Africans in 1813.[146] As a layman, he took the bold step in creating an African Methodism free of white control over ordination and property; developed his own form of church government; set up schools that emphasized instruction of the US Constitution; and encouraged women preachers. By living in Delaware, he was aided by Delaware's laws, that made it easier to establish a religious corporation. Unlike Allen with Bethel, he was not taking any property out of the Methodist Episcopal Church with its Trust Clause restrictions. He started with nothing, except other committed Methodists. He anticipated the future for those Black Methodists and white Methodist Protestants who sought more local control over their ministries than the Methodist Episcopal Church allowed, as descendants of John Wesley's Trust Clause.

Two more substantial developments set the future course for African-American Methodism. The first was Richard Allen in Philadelphia, and the second was the "Zionist" Methodists in New York. Unlike Spencer, they kept the traditional Wesleyan ecclesiology and discipline, with the exception of the trust clause.

To capture the stresses and the turbulence of those times, we need to remember the 1816 General Conference. Tension and sadness filled the air as the clergy delegates gathered in May 1816 in Baltimore. Less than a month earlier, Bishop Asbury had died, which left only Bishop William McKendree (1757-1835) to preside over the General Conference.

On one side was an increasing number of African Americans demanding the right to be traveling preachers with a vote in the

---

146 Lewis V. Baldwin, 'Invisible' Strands of African Methodism: A History of the African Union Methodist Protestant and Union American Churches, 1805-1980. (Scarecrow Press: 1984). Class sizes varied between 25-50 members. It looks like Spencer's class remained with him, while the other class(es) remained or returned to Ezion.

annual conference outside the meeting. The other side was the white "Radical" Methodists seated inside, who clamored: "A Nation Without a King Should Have a Church Without a Bishop." These future Methodist Protestants wanted a democratic Methodist Church without bishops and the laity having voting rights in the annual conference.

Into this boiling cauldron was William McKendree, the only bishop to preside. Earlier in his ministry, he had briefly joined James O'Kelley's 1792 effort to form the Republican Methodist Church. A year later, McKendree returned to the Methodist Episcopal Church. He must have proven himself worthy of election to the Episcopal office in 1808. Now, his job was to preserve the church's unity despite the pressures brought by white democratic Methodists and Black Methodists.

In the end, the 1816 General Conference preserved the status quo. No decisions were made on behalf of either Black or white aspirations for the church to evolve in new ways. With Asbury no longer present to use his mediation skills and the growth of the church westward, the General Conference took care of the business by electing two new bishops: Enoch George and Robert Richford Roberts. This election was the most change the church could accommodate under its present, uncertain situation.

Before the delegates took their seats in Baltimore, Richard Allen, Daniel Coker, and other Black clergy and laity from the Baltimore-Philadelphia area had anticipated the status quo. No Black minister was eligible to speak or offer a vote because a delegate had to be a Traveling Elder. For them, nothing was going to change, so they formed their own church and separated from the Mother Church.

The African Methodist Episcopal Church was born in Philadelphia, twenty-nine years after Bethel Church was built in 1787. The founders had been faithful members of the Methodist Episcopal Church from the beginning of their faith journey. The impact on Black Methodist Episcopal membership in Philadelphia was staggering, with Allen taking 1,296 to Bethel, leaving 75 who later formed Zoar Methodist Episcopal Church.

In April 1816, four Asbury ordained clergy are now local Elders,[147] accompany the Episcopal priest Absalom Jones in the consecration of Richard Allen as bishop. The center of this new church became Mother Bethel Church in Philadelphia. From this time onward, many churches took the name Bethel to ensure their identity as followers of Bishop Allen. This action earned them the name "Allenites."

The distinctions in the names still exist in places like Easton, Maryland. Two African-American churches have existed near one another for over two centuries. One is Bethel African Methodist Episcopal Church (AMEC), and the other is Asbury United Methodist Church. The Easton African Americans who remained in the Methodist Episcopal Church named their church "Asbury" in honor of the first Methodist Episcopal Church bishop, Francis Asbury. Both churches show their debt to the two bishops who were the first in their denomination to hold the office of bishop.

To illustrate how this unfolded in one area is the story of Rev. Shadrack Bassett. He was commissioned as an African Methodist Episcopal missionary and sent to the Eastern Shore of Maryland, where he approached free Black Methodists who already were members of class meetings in the Methodist Episcopal Church.

---

147 Bangs, *History*, 32.

Philadelphia Black Separation

MEMBERS

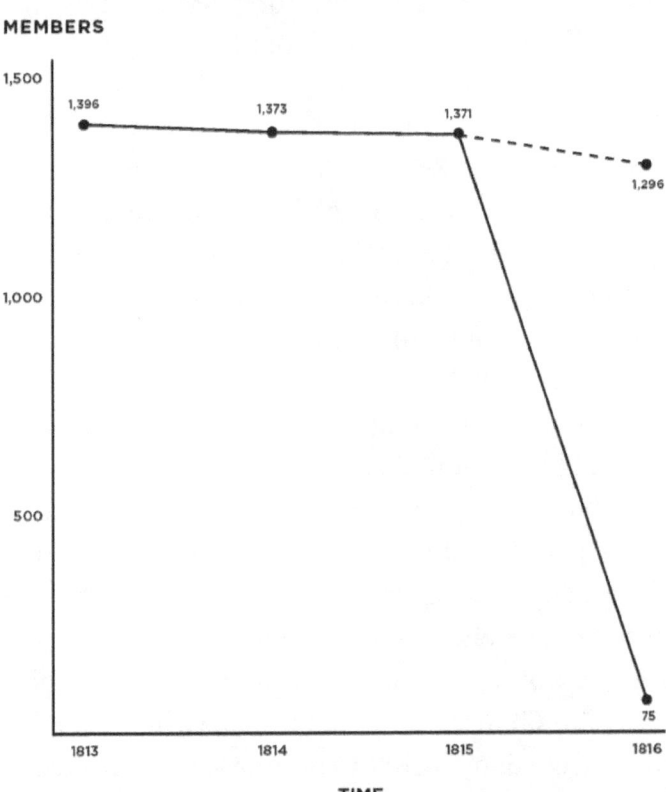

TIME

St. Georges: ———————————————————————

Allen: —

Source: General Minutes, Methodist Episcopal Church, 1813-1816

He gave them a choice of joining the African Methodist Episcopal Church or remain in the Methodist Episcopal Church.

Such a choice was described by the future Bishop Alexander Walker Wayman. He tells how one Methodist Episcopal Church Black local preacher, Samuel Todd, faced this decision:

> The first A.M.E. minister that I heard of who visited the Eastern Shore of Maryland was Rev. Shadrack Bassett. He came over from Baltimore and went to the town of Easton, in Talbot County, and preached under some trees, selecting for his pulpit a cart. He read for his opening hymn, 'Oh! tell me no more of this world's vain store.' And when he came to that verse: 'To dwell I'm determined on that happy ground,' he pointed in a certain direction.
>
> The people thought that he intended to say, there was the place for him to build his Church. And upon that very spot, the first A. M. E. Church of that region was built.
>
> From Easton, Rev. Shadrack Bassett passed up to Caroline County, and stopped at my father's house. Learning that there was a certain local preacher by the name of Samuel Todd, living in another part of the County, and if he could get him [Black Todd] to join his Church, he would have a strong man. My father gave him the direction where to find him. Mr. Bassett started, and after walking some miles he reached Todd's house, and inquired for him. His wife suspected what Mr. Bassett wanted with her husband. She reluctantly told him he was out in the field plough-ing, and he moved off in that direction. When he drew near to Mr. Todd, he said, 'Turn out those oxen;' and by the time he was up to where Mr. Todd was the oxen were unharnessed, and he was ready to go to the house. Samuel Todd then and there agreed to unite with the African M. E. Church. [148]

---

148 James A Handy, *Scraps of African Methodist Episcopal History* (Philadelphia, AME Book Concern, 1902), p. 28 and Bishop Alexander Walker Wayman, *My Recollections*, pp. 1-2.

This choice was acknowledged at the 1878 session of the Delaware Annual Conference of the Methodist Episcopal Church at Waugh Chapel in Cambridge. After the delegation from the African Methodist Episcopal Church had presented greetings to the body, the Rev. W. J. Parker of the Delaware Conference responded graciously:

> "We acknowledge that you went out from us several years ago, and had about sixty years start of us; but during the last fifteen years, we have come alongside of you. We are not prejudiced against you. There is no need of fighting. No, No! I believe it was a good thing for us that the split took place in the Church: it made men industrious; it brought about that enthusiasm amongst men that made them study the interests of the Church. . . So are we; though sailing under different banners, we are all under one Captain."[149]

The next church to be formed was the African Methodist Episcopal Zion Church in New York.[150] Their experience was different from Richard Allen's at St. George's. During his time, St. George's experienced many tugs of war between Africans to Africans, whites to Africans, and whites to whites. At John Street (Wesley Chapel), there was more unity among all the members. When Zion members wanted to have their own building under their control, it was allowed. The most pronounced struggle was between the African Methodists themselves on what they sought to do as Methodists.

---

149 *Delaware Annual Conference Journal,* 1878, p. 15.

150 In 1805, the African Methodist Episcopal Church in America was first used by the Zion Church.

New York Black Separation

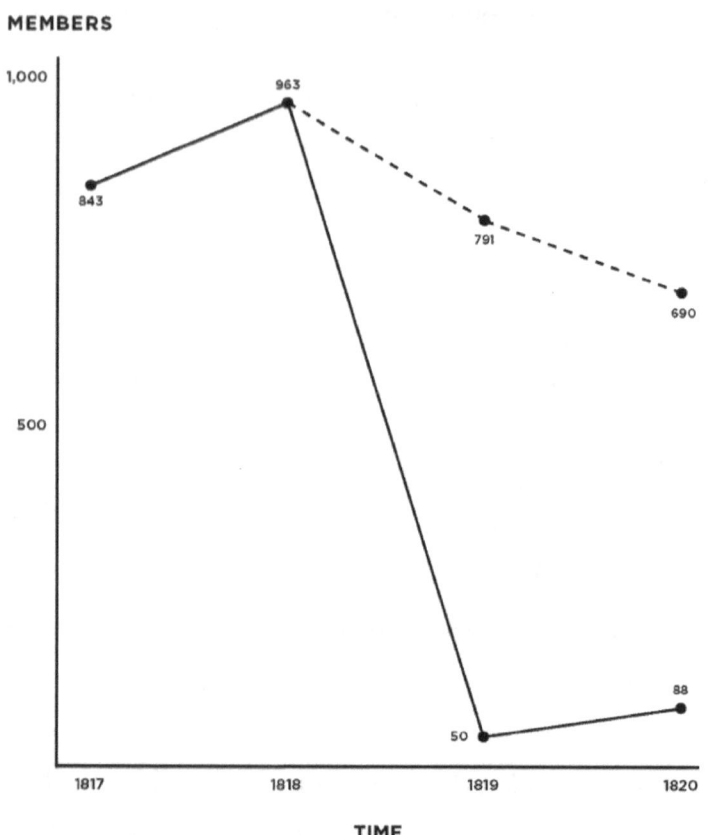

MEMBERS

1,000

963

843

791

690

500

50

88

1817   1818   1819   1820

TIME

John Street: ——————————————

Zion: -

Source: General Minutes, Methodist Episcopal Church, 1817-1820

Shortly after Zion was built, a second church was formed called Asbury, which operated more on the edge of New York African Methodism. Like Allen, the other tension was with the New York Annual Conference over ordination. In spite of their denied aspirations, it did not produce an angry break, like in Philadelphia. Five years later, they had hopes of continuing a relationship with the Methodist Episcopal Church; however, no relationship resulted from that effort. These New York Methodists took the name African Methodist Episcopal Zion Church which identified them as Black, Methodist, and from Zion Church, New York. They became known as "Zionists."

Though the Allenites and Zionists had much in common, each church chose to go her own way over seeking a union.

Though the majority of African Methodists in Philadelphia joined Bethel AME Church, those who remained members of the Methodist Episcopal Church founded Zoar Methodist Episcopal Church. The churn continued in 1820 when about thirty members of Bethel left to form Wesley, a congregation in the African Methodist Episcopal Zion Church. Africans now had the freedom to choose whatever brand of Methodism they wanted, all within walking distance of each other.

This reshuffling and the power to choose one's church was the beginning of a fifty-year development in African Methodism. The majority of African American Methodist members remained members of the Methodist Episcopal Church. The loss of Black members was in the north to these newly developing Black denominations – African Methodist Episcopal Church, African Methodist Episcopal Zion Church, and the Spencer churches. Richard Allen had reached beyond Philadelphia-Baltimore into Black Methodism of Charleston, South

Carolina, where he built a membership of 1,848; however, the majority of approximately 12,000 members remained with the Methodist Episcopal Church. Unfortunately, Allen lost all his members because of the white reaction to Denmark Vesey's attempted Revolt in 1822 to kill the white enslavers and to free the enslaved Blacks. The push-back against the church was severe, and the church was forcibly closed. Overall, during this period, about 80 percent of the African Americans remained members of the Methodist Episcopal Church.

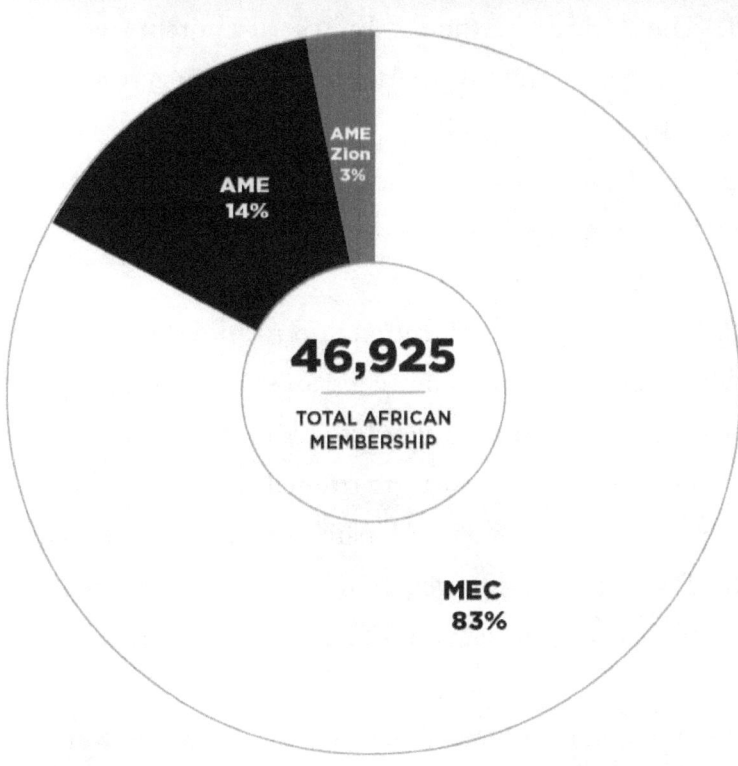

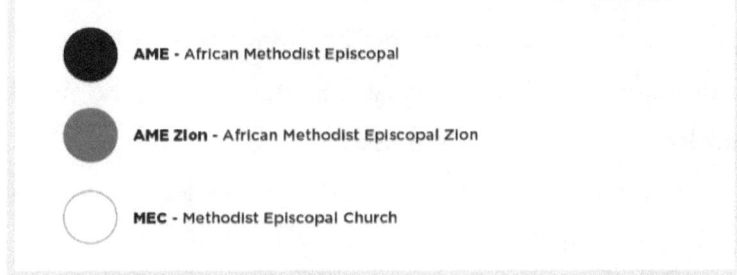

What enabled Richard Allen to succeed in building the African Methodist Episcopal Church, which has survived and thrived for over two hundred years, is the same for the African Methodist Episcopal Zion Church:

1. The African Methodist Episcopal churches were in cities that were committed to African education on a meaningful scale by influential whites.

2. The leaders of the African Methodist Episcopal churches were free Africans and better able to move about and build supportive relationships.

3. From the mix of education and relationships in the African Methodist Episcopal Churches arose very competent leaders who could develop younger leaders to succeed them.

4. The younger leaders were trained in a connectional system, which was a system of leadership development on many levels.

5. The founding congregations had substantial buildings and large enough congregations to be self-supporting.

A congregational system, like a Baptist or that of Rev. Absalom Jones at St. Thomas Episcopal Church, does not need a leadership system beyond the local church. In Rev. Jones' situation, the Episcopal Church controlled the clergy, which determined the number of churches. Rev. Peter Spencer's weaknesses were in the small size of a congregation; no facility; no trained ordained leaders; and, an untried structural system to move the church beyond his region.

The Wesleyan system of leadership development arrived in Philadelphia in 1769. For the next five decades, each African denomination learned how to develop Methodist leaders. Since there was no segregated developmental system at the Quarterly Conference level, they had trained leaders to lead them, when the two churches became independent.

Rev. Noah Colwell W. Cannon is a prime example:

[From Sussex County, Delaware,] I went to Philadelphia and joined the society, and at last I was called on to take charge of a class, from that I passed the quarterly conference for an exhorter, and after that received license to preach and joined the travelling connexion[151] . . .

In the year of 1816, in March 26, I left the Methodist Episcopal Church after this about twelve years. When I joined the African Methodist Episcopal Church, some of my white brethren told me that I had disgraced myself by joining that church, and yet they were not willing to give me a chance to do what the Lord had commanded me, but I understand that, you shall not muzzle.[152] . . a certain gentleman who called himself a lawyer, I being in company with him he swore in my presence and I took him to task for it, and he said I suppose you are one of the Methodists who say it is wrong to swear; I answered and said that I was a Methodist, and he said that he believed I was a liar. 1 then pulled out a Methodist Discipline to prove to him that I was[153] ...'

Rev. Canon[154] had experienced Wesleyan system: member of a society, a class leader, an exhorter, a licensed preacher, and an itinerant

---

151 Rev Noah C.W. Cannon, *Book of Wisdom,* page 38-39. https://archive.org/details/bookofwisdomgreeOOdeanrich

152 Ibid, page 123.

153 Ibid, page 39.

154 Founded Charles Street AMEC in Boston and died at age 64 in Canonsburg, Canada, which bore his name. Wayman, *Cyclopedia,* page 33.

minister. He even carried a Methodist Discipline with him! Effortlessly, he went from the Methodist Episcopal Church to the African Methodist Episcopal Church, because the systems functioned the same.

CHAPTER 14

African-Americans Respond to the Southern Methodist Outreach

A decade later, the ministry to unchurched Africans in the South was changing, too. The preacher who propelled this mission was the Rev. William Capers, presiding elder of the Charleston District, South Carolina Annual Conference. In 1825 Capers' district counted 3,492 White and 5,917 Black members, which did not count enslaved and unchurched Africans on remote plantations. In 1829, Capers created a program to reach out to them by enlisting ordained clergy to be full-time missionaries to Africans on remote plantations.

Two missions to plantation African slaves were established: South of Ashley River, to which the Rev. John Honour was appointed missionary, and the Santee River was served by the Rev. J. H. Massey. In addition to his regular duties as Presiding Elder, Capers was appointed the Superintendent of these two missions.[155] Rev. Honour

155 William M. Wightman, *Life of William Capers*, (Publishing House of the MECS, 1902), page 292.

died within a month of starting this ministry, probably from malaria. Being exposed to malaria in Africa may have given the Africans a kind of immunity. In spite of the setback, in their first year, these two missions gathered 417 new members.[156]

In keeping with the Wesleyan "methodical" approach to organization, Capers developed two catechisms for children and youth, known as the *Caper Catechisms*. They were used across the South and taught basic Christian religious instruction as well as English. For many Africans, these catechisms were their first formal educational experience. For a few African American students, this was the first step in becoming a Methodist local preacher.

Even the fierce white backlash to Nat Turner's Rebellion did not halt this work. In a counter intuitive way it had the effect of justifying the continuance of Capers' African outreach. The Rev. James O. Andrew alluded to both as he presented a resolution at the 1832 anniversary of the Missionary Society:

> That, while we consider false views of religion as being every way mischievous, and judge from the past that much evil has resulted from the cause among the slave population of this country, we are fully persuaded that it is not only safe, but highly expedient to society at large, to furnish the slaves as fully as possible with the means of true spiritual instruction and the worship of God.[157]

In time this ministry spread to the other Methodist annual conferences across the South. Twenty-five years later, Bishop Holland

---

156 Ibid, page 294.
157 Holland N. McTyerie, *History of Methodism* (Nashville: Publishing House MECS, 1916), page 585.

N. McTyerie,[158] who had been one of Caper's missionaries, recorded:

> Nearly a generation has passed away since the commencement of these missionary operations among the Blacks. It is interesting to trace their expansion and results through a quarter of a century. That there has been a large development is proved by the statistics published from year to year by the Missionary Society. In 1833 two additional mission stations were established. In 1834, they numbered six; in 1835, eight; in 1836, nine; 1837, ten; and ten years afterwards, viz., in 1847, there were seventeen missions, served by twenty—five efficient preachers of the Conference. By the death of Bishop Capers, there were twenty—six missionary stations in South Carolina, on which were employed thirty—two preachers. The number of Church members at that time was 11,546 on three mission stations.[159]

Though the 1844 division of the Methodist Episcopal Church over slavery will be discussed in more detail later, keep in mind that he is reporting is ten years later, and the northern church conducted no new outreach to African Americans. McTyerie reported additional statistics and concluded with this statement.

> These results are separate from the negro membership distributed in smaller numbers through the upper country, and more accessible by the regular pastors. The Kentucky Conference, which reported in 1846 but one mission to the colored people, numbered among its regular communicants 9,479 of this class;

---

158 The activities of Bishop McTyrie, Bishop Paine, and others, who served as missionaries to African Americans on remote plantations, have been suppressed in the telling of their lives in Post-Civil War America.

159 Ibid, page 297.

and the Holston Conference made a report of no mission, but reckoned a colored membership of 4,133. The rule laid down by the South Carolina Board: "That, as a general rule for our circuits and station, we deem it best to include the colored people in the same pastoral charge with the whites, and to preach to both classes in one congregation, as our practice has been. The gospel is the same for all men, and to enjoy its privileges in common promotes goodwill. That at all preaching places where galleries or other suitable sittings have not been provided for the colored people, or where the galleries or other sittings are insufficient, we consider it the duty of our brethren and friends to provide the necessary accommodations, that none may make such a neglect a plea for absenting themselves from public worship."[160]

How did these isolated African Americans respond to these Southern Methodist missionaries? They took the hand offered to them and made the best of it. African-American parents brought their children to the catechetical instruction classes to learn about the Christian faith, which was taught everywhere orally.[161]

Adult male African Americans were trained and enlisted by Capers into a corps to promote the welfare of their brothers and sisters. In Fayetteville, North Carolina, he found Henry Evans, a shoemaker from Virginia; Castile Selby and John Boquet of Charleston; Will Campbell and Harry Myrick of Wilmington, NC; York Cohen of Savannah; and from Charleston: Amos Baxter, Tom Smith, Peter Simpson, Smart Simpson, Harry Bull, Richard Holloway, and Alex Harlston.[162]

Methodism was so important to them that when they moved from one plantation to another these Black enslaved Methodists became their own self-appointed missionaries:

160 Ibid, page 587.
161 Ibid, page 300.
162 Ibid, page 106.

...then there were those times when the Methodist missionary preacher arrived for the first time on a plantation and found a Methodist society already organized with times of worship, structure and members by the slaves themselves who had come from a plantation where there existed a Methodist ministry. A Louisiana missionary found an existing society of thirty members![163]

For these African Americans, it was their Methodist ministry

This Southern African missionary enterprise was seen as integral to the mission of the whole church. To illustrate the stature of this ministry, two former missionaries were later elected bishops: Robert Paine and Holland McTyerie. Their connection was to African American Methodists was so close that after the Civil War, they ordained and consecrated W.H. Miles and R.H. Vanderhorst as the first two bishops of the Colored Methodist Episcopal Church in 1870. The Colored (now Christian) Methodist Episcopal Church is the only independent Black Methodist church to experience the unbroken laying on of hands from the first bishops of American Methodism, Francis Asbury and Thomas Coke, to their bishops. Richard Allen and James Varick were not consecrated as bishops by another bishop but by Elders.

After Bishop William Capers' death, his friends had inscribed on his tombstone, "Founder of the Mission to the Slaves,"[164] and a great chorus of Southern African-American Methodists shouted: 'AMEN!'

---

163 Ibid, page 589.

164 William M. Wightman, *Life of William Capers*, (Publishing House of the MECS, 1902), 491.

Bishop James O. Andrew

Born 1794 in Wilkes County, Georgia
Died 1871
Elected Bishop 1832 (age 36)
1844 - 'The Bishop in the Middle'

CHAPTER 15

1844: A Line is Drawn

In the midst of a polarized America, the 1844 General Conference delegates gathered in New York City. As the people
assembled for their meeting, the focus was on one subject: Could
a slaveholding Southern bishop preside over the conferences in the
North? Though this was about African Americans, no Black
Americans were seated within the bar of the conference to voice
their position. How the Conference answered this question would
be answered by the white Methodists. The debate was intense as the
delegates verbally punched hard with parliamentary feints and jabs
for over a month. No one held back.

The Abolition Movement was the fire driving the debate. Abolition
was the conviction that slaves should be freed immediately without
compensation to their owners. Abolitionism had now reached fever
pitch in America and the Methodist Episcopal Church.

The General Conference from 1784 onward, before the U.S.
Constitution was adopted, had taken strong positions against

slaveholding but not on abolition. Over time, compromises were made with Methodists who owned slaves. Though many Methodist preachers were against slaveholding, especially the business of selling slaves, they felt abolition was too extreme. Even the U.S. Constitution failed to treat African-American slaves as citizens. Underlying the argument was the American economy. The Southern economy was based on the industrial production of cotton for the global market. The slave-owners made significant upfront investments in slave labor to meet the world's demand. In return, their investment brought them incredible profits without the need for tariffs.

The northern economy was local and national. The North had not developed the industrial scale to compete on a global scale and needed tariff protection from British industry. Their workforce came from the increasing influx of European immigrants who worked for cheap wages and had no upfront 'investment,' like the slave economy.

For the northern economy, slavery was no longer an option because its economy could no longer support it. The states then began outlawing slavery. Though the North no longer needed slavery, freed Black Americans earned little in competition with the immigrants and racial prejudice kept them isolated and devoid of civil rights. They were economically pushed to the margins of working society. No one wanted to invest in their labor with hungry immigrants entering America every day from Europe.

For both sides at the General Conference, abolition was an economic issue. The North understood slavery solely as a moral issue without an economic plan to pay for the transition to a wage economy from a slave economy. For the South without slave labor, there was no prosperity.

At the General Conference, this conflict was brought to bear on one man, the Southern Bishop, James O. Andrew. He was a personification of the debate on the abolition of slavery. It was not a debate over his character, because he was not in violation of the Book of Discipline nor guilty of a crime. Since the General Conference elected him, he had married a woman with slaves. He had not bought nor sold a slave. In the eyes of his opposition, he was a slaveholder, and this would disqualify him from being able to discharge his Episcopal duties as the presiding bishop over a northern annual conference.

In Andrew's defense, the southern delegates pointed out that Georgia law made those slaves his against his will and the law forbade him from freeing them. By marrying his wife, he became by state law the owner of the slaves. Earlier, he had owned a female slave whom he tried to free. She would not leave him, because the state required as a condition of her freedom that she leave the state or go to Liberia.[165]

It was the practice of the Council of Bishops to make their own assignments over which conferences they would preside over in a given year. Assignments were not in the jurisdiction of an annual conference nor General Conference. With the distances involved, bishops no longer traveled outside of the larger area in which they lived. Even then, they often spent nine months away from home. Practically speaking, Bishop Andrew would never be assigned to a northern annual conference, nor a northerner to the south.

Besides state law, Bishop Andrew could not surmount the political and economic interests dividing the two sections of the country. The

---

165 A recent story appeared *The Washington Post* (February 3, 2024) illustrating the impossibility of remaining a free Black in the South. The article talked about William and Ellen Craft who were both slaves. She, being light-skinned, posed as a man and William, as 'his' slave. They escaped North and then to England to escape the grip of Fugitive Slave Act (1793, 1850).

northerners saw the tariffs as a necessity for their prosperity, and the South understood it as a tax in support of the North. The volatility had spilled over a decade earlier. Southern wealth with its hatred of tariffs had propelled the South close to a civil war over the Nullification Issue, whereby a state could nullify a federal law.

Another issue that added fuel to the sectional fire was the power of the three-fifths clause in the Constitution. Slaves were counted as 3/5th in the federal census for establishing the number of representatives in the House of Representatives. The North resented the power it gave to the South because of the preponderance of southern slaves. The North felt that only whites should be counted in the census.[166] Counting slaves who were not citizens gave the South more power over the congressional budget than the North.

To grasp the political impact on how to count slaves, consider the consequences of the 14th Amendment. Those once three-fifths slaves became five-fifths citizens. When the South rejoined the Union, it gained forty more electoral votes with its free African-American citizens. Southern power returned to the House of Representatives. It is interesting to consider that had the South been able to amend the Constitution from three-fifths to five-fifths, the South would have retained its congressional power and wealth without the Civil War. Of course, the North would not approve such an amendment.

Returning to the 1844 General Conference, the first resolution "affectionally requested [him] to resign his office as one of the Bishops of the Methodist Episcopal Church." Later, it was softened to ask him to "desist from the exercise of this office so long as this impediment

---

166 At the Constitutional Convention, the South wanted slaves counted the same as whites for purposes of representation, not as voting citizens.

remains."[167] The final vote was sectional, with the northern majority voting 111 in favor and the southern 69 (total of 180). There was never any doubt who had the votes to win. Ironically, earlier Bishop Andrew had given serious consideration to resigning his office with its burdensome financial demands and the need to be away nine months a year.

In reality, had Bishop Andrew stepped aside as the resolution requested, the conference would have been powerless to find a replacement for him. After such a display before all the delegates, no northerner would have been acceptable to the south, and the north had already declared no southerner was acceptable to them. No answer could keep the church together and the north sought none. One northern bishop thought the decision was unfair, Bishop Joshua Soule. He left the Northern body and joined the Southern church.

The bottom line was that the northern delegates knew they had the votes and were determined to overturn the Methodist practice of abiding by state law regarding a Methodist owning slaves. They drew a bold line of separation against the South, even if it meant the end of the unified Methodist Episcopal Church. The time for arguments and compromises had ended with the church divided. Unlike the 1861 American Southern Secession, it was the northern Methodists who moved to force the Southern Methodists out of the church.

The question must be asked: Why were these northern delegates unconcerned with losing 83 percent of their African American members to a separate Southern Methodist church? The irony of the 1844 division of the Methodist Episcopal Church is that the Methodist Episcopal Church, South, became the largest African American

---

167 A. H. Redford, *History of the Organization of the Methodist Episcopal Church, South,* (Nashville: A. H. Redford, 1871), 313.

church in the United States. Consequentially, the northern Methodist Episcopal Church became the white Methodist Episcopal Church with its African American presence only at its southernmost mid-Atlantic edges.[168] Sixteen years later, the General Minutes of the Methodist Episcopal Church reported the number of African members as zero, while South Carolina's African membership was 39,495.

The year before the 1844 Conference, the General Minutes of the Methodist Episcopal Church had 1,021,918 white members and 150,120 African American members. Five years after the 1844 separation, the General Conference of the Northern Methodist Episcopal Church listed only 26,309 Black members.

One year after the Methodist Episcopal Church split over the issue of abolition and slaveholding, the South had 124,000 enslaved Africans as members. Fifteen years later, the total would increase to 207,766 plus 180,000 children under catechetical instruction through the missionary efforts of Capers and other interested southern Methodists.

At the same time, another line was being drawn across American society: scientific racism. The status of people of African descent was being re-imagined by white scholars. Robert Elder in Calhoun: *An American Heretic* described it this way:

In the 1830s scholars started discarding environment theories of race and adopted a scientific approach with harder lines of distinction between the races. Cranial capacity theories of

---

168 Twenty years earlier its Northern Black membership left to form independent de-nominations. The remaining Black Methodists would become in 1864, the Delaware and Washington Annual Conferences. They represent the only full historical and institutional continuity of Black Methodism within "Mother Methodism" from 1784 to the present.

Professor of Anatomy Samuel George Morton at Pennsylvania Medical College and Charles Caldwell of the University of Pennsylvania argued that Africans were an inferior strand of the human race. By 1835 these ideas had entered into popular discourse.

The theory that the Negro was incapable of being civilized or enjoying freedom as whites was supported by scholars on both sides of the Atlantic. Josiah Knot and George Glidden argued Africans were a separate and inferior species in *Four Types of Mankind* (1854). Famous scientific figures of the day, like Harvard's Louis Agassi, claimed that Black racial inferiority is a scientific fact. This brushed away what earlier Americans in the late eighteenth century believed, that over time, Blacks could become accomplished and equal to whites. This new scientific reasoning took this cultural understanding of eventual equality off the table and replaced it with the 'scientific facts' of eugenics.

This new modern mindset was placed on top of the economic 'experience' that slavery was a necessary building block of progress. Slavery's proponents pointed to the examples of the American South, Cuba, and Brazil as places of prosperity because of slavery. Then, these proponents pointed to countries without slavery whose economies languished, like Mexico and other South American countries.[169]

As northern Methodists and scholars were distancing themselves from Black people, a surprise was waiting for them as they gathered for the next General Conference by Blacks who were unwilling to go quietly into the night.

---

169 Robert Elder, "It is our Thermopylae" *Calhoun: An American Heretic.* (New York: Basic Books, 2021).

Bishop Levi Scott

Born 1802 in Odessa, Delaware
Died 1882
Elected Bishop 1852 (age 50)
Convener of First Colored Preachers Conference

CHAPTER 16

Africans Decide Their Future: As Equals

If the purpose of the northern delegates of the 1844 General Conference was to rid the church of slaveholding bishops, it had an unintended consequence. The remaining Black members in the Baltimore and Philadelphia Annual Conferences now wanted their own annual conferences to be equal to the white conferences.

To the white delegates, these northern African American Methodists were inconsequential in number themselves. The white delegates had no desire to elevate their Black members beyond the historic control of the quarterly conference. The northern and southern Methodists operated the same way they had always behaved since the beginning. The times were changing. Prejudice blinded them from wanting to accommodate the concerns of their Black members, who sought to move beyond the quarterly conference to an annual conference of their own.

For these Black churchmen and women, the Methodist Episcopal Church was their church. They did not walk out to join the newly established independent Black Methodist denominations located in Baltimore, Philadelphia, New York, and Wilmington, Delaware. Within the church that had from the beginning welcomed them, they now sought to find an equal place within the church whereby their full privileges as members could be exercised to the fullest extent.

1848

With the southern delegates no longer present to thwart their aspirations, these Black clergy seized the opportunity to push for their own annual conference within the Methodist Episcopal Church. Leaders from Sharp Street and Asbury churches in Baltimore, Philadelphia, and New Jersey submitted their resolutions to the 1848 General Conference meeting in Pittsburgh. It was a bold act to get a proper hearing, since no Blacks had the right to vote or to serve on a committee to advocate for their cause.

Their advocacy for an equal annual conference revealed the hypocrisy of the General Conference. In the past northerners understood themselves as taking the high moral ground against slavery and passing resolutions advocating for abolition and supporting the return of free Africans to Liberia, Africa, through the colonization movement. Outside the deliberations of the body, their own Black members sought to have a place at the table and refused to support the return to Africa effort. America was their home and the Methodist Episcopal Church was their church. They were successful in getting the Conference to take action on their proposal.

The Conference had formed a committee of five clergy from Baltimore, Philadelphia, New Jersey, New York, and Illinois. On

May 23, 1848, they reported to the plenary session the results of their deliberations:

> The committee to whom were referred memorials (resolutions) from the Sharp Street and Asbury station of coloured members in the city of Baltimore, and from various coloured societies in Pennsylvania, New Jersey, and Delaware, asking for the organization of annual conferences of coloured traveling preachers, under the supervision of our bishops, beg leave to report:
>
> That having carefully considered the memorials, and feeling an earnest desire to do all that can be done to promote the spiritual interest of our coloured people, they recommend to the General Conference, for adoption, the following resolutions:
>
> *Resolved,* 1. That the organization of such annual conference is inexpedient at present.
>
> *Resolved,* 2. That the Discipline be so amended that the 5th answer in section 10, part 2, shall read as follows: 'The bishops may employ coloured preachers to travel and preach, where their services are judged necessary; provided that no one shall be so employed without having been recommended by a quarterly conference.'[170]

There was no ambiguity in their unwillingness to grant them permission to create their own annual conference. Their only concession was the smallest of the possible small. It allowed for the possibility of a Black preacher to become a 'traveling' preacher within a quarterly conference outside his own, provided that the bishop believed the preacher was qualified and there was a need. The words "may employ" are far from "shall employ."

---

170 *Proceedings of General Conference Methodist Episcopal Church,* May 23, 1848 session.

Black Local Preachers had always traveled around their quarterly conference. This decision gave the possibility to have a bishop assign a Black Local Preacher to another quarterly conference and designate him as a 'traveling local preacher.' This was already done by presiding elders who needed a Black preacher in a neighboring conference. This practice can now be elevated to a bishop who changes the annual conference yearly. This was only window dressing. The Black preacher remained in lay status and the title was conditional; whereas, a white ordained traveling elder held the title of traveling until he relinquished it.

The conference's decision was not what they wanted, but it was a public recognition of the value and competency of the Black preacher expressed in the title "traveling." Though he was not going to travel far, the word "traveling" was an acceptance that had never been bestowed before on a Black Methodist preacher.

The attention of the General Conference was on establishing German annual conferences in the United States and supporting the sending of free Blacks to Africa. It was not in granting her faithful Black members the opportunity to establish their own annual conference.

May 1852

Four years later, the 1852 General Conference met in Boston. This time, Black leaders were from the Philadelphia Annual Conference, possibly David Tilghman, who once lived in Boston. The request was the same: a petition for their own annual conference. This time, they were able to push the door open just a crack. The

General Conference gave them permission to hold their own annual meeting (not an annual conference) under the direction of a bishop.

Here is how it was reported in the official proceedings:

The Committee on Missions reported, in part, as follows, was adopted: —

The Committee on Missions, to whom was referred the Coloured preachers petition of the coloured brethren from Philadelphia, asking that the pastors within the Philadelphia and New-Jersey and New Jersey conferences may be formed into an Annual Conference, under the supervision of the Bishops and of the Presiding Elders of said Conferences, within whose bounds their (the coloured pastors') work may lie, beg leave to report-

That the Committee have given due consideration to the said petition, and have heard the bearers of it in person, and have obtained all information within their reach, and have come to the following conclusions:

First. That it is very desirable that the coloured pastors, mentioned in the petition aforesaid, should have an opportunity to meet together once a year, in the presence or under the supervision of the Bishop, or Bishops, in order to confer together with respect to the best means of promoting their work, and to receive the assignment of their work from the Bishop, to the churches usually left in the minutes 'to be supplied.'

Second. That in this meeting it is desirable that the Presiding Elders, in whose bounds the coloured churches and congregations lie, should be present to assist the Bishop in assigning the work.

Third, Provided, upon due inquiry by the Bishops, they shall find a sufficient number of coloured preacher, sufficient qualifications to justify an annual meeting.

Having arrived at these conclusions, the Committee has agreed on the following resolution, which is reported for adoption by the General Conference:

Resolved, That we advise that the coloured local preachers now employed, or who may be employed, within the bounds of the Philadelphia and New-Jersey Annual Conferences, be assembled together once in each year, by the Bishop or Bishops, who may preside in said Conference, for bounds and under whose care the coloured churches and congregations are, be present, and aid the Bishop or Bishops in said annual meeting of coloured local preachers: provided, that upon due inquiry the said Bishop or Bishops shall find such annual meeting aforesaid to be practicable and expedient.[171]

At that time, the church had only three veteran bishops to cover the country with twenty-nine annual conferences. By the time the conference ended, four new bishops were elected which brought the number to seven. It was still a small group to travel across the country to preside over multi-day conferences and handle all the issues bubbling up through the system throughout the year. This was an overtaxed group who traveled many months a year away from home. It is fair to assume the white delegates did not think much was going to happen from the change they had created. What bishop would find the time to fit another multi-day conference into his schedule?

The annual meeting was a welcome change; however, it was accompanied by another indignity: it was unilaterally stated that no ordained African American clergyman would be elected bishop in the United States.[172] To have a Black man elected bishop in the United States meant the possibility of presiding over a white

---

171 *Proceedings of the 1852 General Conference Methodist Episcopal Church*, 1852, p. 65.
172 1852 *Proceedings of General Conference*, page 193-194.

annual conference, as bishops rotated among the various white annual conferences. When Francis Burns, an African American clergyman, was elected as the bishop for Liberia in 1858, it was on the condition that he could only preside in Liberia as a missionary bishop. Africa was as close to America these delegates could tolerate.

Upon hearing this decision, a Southern Methodist correspondent for the *Nashville and Louisville Christian Advocate* (a Southern Methodist publication) derived satisfaction from being able to report that his Northern brethren were faced with "quite a dilemma." He quipped that allowing a Black bishop to "claim an equal part" in church government would have made "abolitionism a little too practical, even for them, though consistency would make them swallow the pill."[173] They could not tolerate in 1844 a white slave-holding bishop, and in 1852, a Black bishop was intolerable, too.

These Black leaders still pushed ahead with fortitude and three months later called a convention in Philadelphia. It was called a 'convention' instead of a 'conference,' because it was their own planning meeting to prepare for the later promised conference meeting. This convention was to demonstrate their ability to create a fully functioning annual conference. They were shouting – "We are ready!"

August 1852

On Monday, August 23, 1852, the first meeting of the Black clergy convention gathered at Zoar Church, Philadelphia, with no bishop nor presiding elder present.[174] They chose Ely Nugent,

173 *Nashville and Louisville Christian Advocate,* June 3, 1852. Quoted by Reginald F. Hildebrand, *Methodist Episcopal Policy on the Ordination of Black Ministers, 1784-1864. Methodist History.* page 136.

174 L.Y. Cox, *Pioneer Footsteps,* Star and Wave Press: Cape May, NJ, 1917.

pastor of Asbury Church in Washington, D.C., as their chair. Born free in nearby Montgomery County, Maryland, Nugent had been a member of the Foundry Methodist Episcopal Church and was ordained in the 1830s. Like many Black Methodists, he was restless to exercise his gifts of ministry beyond the restrictions imposed upon them by the General Conference. Within Foundry's Circuit and Quarterly Conference, he helped found the Asbury Methodist Episcopal Church. He became active in the civic community, too. When the Washington Colored Sabbath School Union was formed in 1844 to promote Sabbath Schools for Black people, Nugent was unanimously elected as a vice president and his son, Ely Nugent Jr., was elected treasurer. He was so highly esteemed that when he died, the U.S. Supreme Court adjourned to attend his funeral.[175]

In good Methodist fashion, they began with the organization of the body with the election of officers: Rev. Nugent as President, Rev. Issac Hinson as Vice-President, and Rev. David Tilghman as Secretary. Other clergy included Jacob Erving [Delaware County], Henry Nelson [Port Deposit], Peter Wise (Philadelphia), Noah Fisher [Philadelphia], Richard Crawford (Philadelphia), and James Davis, and laity were Smith Seaman (New Jersey) and Jacob Bradly (Philadelphia).

The 1852 General Conference Resolution was read by Rev. Hinson and received by the body with these attached resolutions:

That we advise the best measures to sustain the resolution.

That all the officers and members of the Methodist Episcopal Church shall have privilege to speak and vote on all questions.

---

175 "Association of Oldest Inhabitants," *Washington Bee*, December 28, 1912.

That each brother shall furnish himself with a proper document, containing the number of members in their respective places of labor, to present to the annual meeting in the spring of 1853.

On Tuesday, when they gathered at 10 a.m., they were joined by Rev. James Davis and by laity, King Still and Philip Hacket. The first order of business was to schedule the time for preaching and a prayer meeting that day. The hour was set for 8:00 p.m.

Rev. Davis introduced the necessity of the preachers volunteering themselves to travel in the itineracy of the Methodist system. After much debate, the following was adopted: that all the preachers volunteer themselves to support the annual meeting to be formed in the spring of 1853.

Rev. Davis also put forward the resolution that all the preachers come recommended by their quarterly conference. This resolution failed to receive enough votes. The reason may stem from white resistance to this effort of becoming equals as Methodists.

The body elected Rev. Wise as Vice-President on the recommendation of Rev. Hinson. Before the meeting closed with a benediction, the body affirmed that they sit with 'open doors. This meant the doors were open for all to attend. This was not a secret meeting. They wanted all to see how capable they were in conducting their business. This was in line with the customary practice in the Black church at the end of the service for the preacher to 'open the doors of the church.' This meant you were welcome to become a member.

On the third day, Wednesday, August 25, after singing and praying, they were joined by Henry Thomas, Harrison Smith, and Issac

Cannon. Rev. Hinson nominated Rev. Thomas for Assistant Secretary. The work of the conference continued with the passage of the following resolutions:

That we take up missionary collections in our circuits and stations, to support our ensuring annual meeting.

That this convention recommend that the quarterly conference appoint a missionary to travel and preach and take up collections throughout the connection.

That a committee of three be appointed to nominate a suitable person as missionary. The names of the committee are: Rev. James Davis, Rev. Issac Hinson, and laity, Henry Thomas. They nominated Rev. Richard Crawford.

For the afternoon session in the absence of Rev. Nugent, Rev Hinson was in the chair who entertained the following changes in the morning resolutions:

- That there be a collection taken on the last sabbath in every month for the support of the missionary.
- That the steward of each circuit or station be appointed to hold money collected for the missionary purpose by each preacher in charge.
- That this convention forwarded a letter to Bishop Janes, to know when the annual meeting of the colored local preachers shall be held.

On the fourth day, Thursday, August 26, Rev. Nugent was back in the presiding officer's chair. Brothers Carter and Curtis joined them for the proceedings. The issue of the missionary was brought up again. You can imagine how these after-hours discussions took place among all the members over who would fill the position and how the new position would be funded, since they had to find funding themselves. Here are the resolutions passed that day:

That if the missionary now recommended to the quarterly conference, sees proper to travel forthwith, that this convention advise him to go into the work.

That the Secretary of this convention forward a letter to the Bishop to [let him] know all the particulars respecting the annual meeting, and to receive the answer (about when and where the first Annual Colored Preachers Meeting was to be held) and inform the brethren.

That brother Henry Nelson be appointed a missionary to operate in the Southern part of the Philadelphia Conference, in conjunction with Brother Crawford.

Other business:
- That the preachers at this convention form themselves into a society, called the "Preachers Aid Society" (to help infirmed clergy and their families. This was an expression of being connected in ministry).
- That there be a committee of three to draught a constitution for the "Preachers Aid Society." [This committee was appointed and was composed of Harrison Smith, Daniel Carter, and Richard Crawford.]
- That this convention pray the sisters (women of the church) to contribute to the aid of their society.
- That this convention authorize the preacher in charge, with the trustees, to appoint a committee to wait on the Bishop, if it is needful.

They approved the publishing of the transactions of the convention, published in the *Christian Advocate*[176] *and Journal* and five hundred copies in pamphlet form. The following were tasked with this job: James I. Davis, Issac Hinson, Harrison Smith, Henry Thomas, Daniel Carter, Jacob Bradley, and Peter Fitterman.

On Friday, August 24, Brother Henry Dobson (listed in Easton Circuit, Kings Creek Class, 1847) joined the meeting. Affirming the decision to print the minutes in pamphlet form, they reduced the editorial committee to three persons: David Tilghman, Henry Thomas, and Peter Wise. After much discussion, they decided to meet again at Zoar in Philadelphia and moved -

> That whereas, the preachers and members of this convention have been together for several days in peace and harmony, we pray that the blessing of God may rest upon all our doings.

They conducted themselves as full Methodists who understood the connectional structure and how to properly conduct the business of a conference. To anyone who has been at today's annual conference sessions, it all sounded very familiar!

August 1857

What was to be their 'meeting to prepare for the meeting for next year's (1853) conference' with the bishop and the presiding elders did not happen. Frustratedly, for these Black leaders, it was going to be five more years before Bishop Levi Scott took the chair for the first of the next six colored local preachers' conferences meeting in Philadelphia and Wilmington, Delaware.

---

176 This was the official Methodist Episcopal publication.

Bishop Scott, who of the bishops lived the closest to Philadelphia, had a strong affection for Black people. Converted in a Black woman's home near his in Odessa, Delaware, he was tasked to travel to Liberia to evaluate the situation after his election as bishop in 1852. This made him the first bishop to visit Africa.

With great anticipation, Bishop Scott called the meeting to order on Wednesday, August 5, 1857. After scripture, prayer, and the bishop's address, he explained the nature of the business before them. As directed by the General Conference, he was joined with the Appointive Cabinet (Districts) of the Philadelphia Conference: North Philadelphia, Rev. P. Coombe; South Philadelphia, W. Cooper; Wilmington, W. Urie; Easton, W. McCombs; Burlington, New Jersey, G. F. Brown; and Bridgeton, New Jersey, S. Y. Monroe.

Rev. Coombe was elected secretary, and Rev. David Tilghman was his assistant. A finance committee was approved to collect funds to pay for the cost of the conference. The bishop called for the statistics on the churches. The conference approved the printing of the minutes. The new traveling preachers would be required to take the Course of Study required by the General Conference.

That evening, in honor of this special occasion, the Ladies of Zoar prepared a special dinner for Bishop Scott and the conference.

The next day, the Conference recommended that all preachers appointed by the bishop secure a copy and study of the *Holy Scriptures, Hymnbook, Discipline, Fletcher's Appeal,* Wesley's sermons, and Hart's *English Grammar.*

Money was approved to purchase a book to keep the minutes of the meetings. The preachers decided to take up a collection of money at all appointments for aiding needy preachers (Preachers' Aid Society). Then, they voted on where to meet next year and the date. David Tilghman was elected treasurer with the authority to collect funds and pay expenses.

Once the Colored Local Preachers Conference met in 1857 in Philadelphia, these leaders demonstrated their readiness to establish their own annual conference within the Methodist Episcopal Church. They dutifully met annually and built an annual conference structure for Black Methodists.

The concluding act of the 1857 conference was Bishop Scott reading the appointment list, assigning the preachers to their churches. This was the first time in the seventy-three-year history of the Methodist Episcopal Church that African American clergy received an appointment for ministry from a presiding bishop! Now, Black clergy, instead of being assigned to a preaching assignment by a presiding elder in a quarterly conference, joined their white Methodist clergy in being appointed by a bishop.

What was being developed among Black Methodists was rare among Methodists, other Christian groups, and in America itself. This started to catch the attention of a much wider audience: Revere Street Methodist Episcopal Church in Boston sent greetings and later asked for help in the Boston Mission. The abolitionist, Rev. William Brisbane, came from his home in Wisconsin to offer his benediction. The local preachers from Baltimore and Washington, Benjamin Brown, Richard P. Bell, F. Bagger and Ely Nugent came to learn from the sessions, as they put plans together to organize the Washington Conference.

One man came from Cambridge, Maryland—Richard Moore, a blacksmith by trade and local Methodist preacher. He had earlier created a stir in Dorchester County and across the United States after he had given Rev. Samuel Green, a local Methodist preacher, a copy of *Uncle Tom's Cabin*. Rev. Green was arrested and given a ten-year jail sentence. Seeking his release from prison became a national cause for abolitionists.

Rev. William Colloday Robinson, a white preacher from the Dover Circuit, expressed the unanimous desire of his Black members to have the services of a Black preacher.

To ascertain who was willing to devote themselves full-time to the work and receive appointments, a roll was taken by the assembled clergy. These men offered themselves for service: James Davis, Richard Crawford, Rodger O. Adams, Issac Hinson, William P. Gibson, John Fisher, John Brown, Philip Scott, Harrison Smith, Samuel Midcap, Samuel Dale, and Joshua Brinkley.

James Davis asked if this conference would ordain local preachers as deacons and elders. The bishop replied that the General Conference had not given this body the authority to perform ordinations. That would change after the 1860 General Conference.

1858 - 1863

With Bishop Scott presiding along with the Presiding Elders, the Colored Preachers Conferences continued yearly and developed a fully functioning structure of an annual conference. The next step was taking this annual meeting and giving it full status as an annual conference in the Methodist Episcopal Church, along with and equal to all other conferences.

1864

The years of work had not been in vain. The country was rapidly changing with Lincoln's Emancipation Proclamation and the enlistment of Black soldiers to fight and die for their country. The Union had defeated the Confederacy at Vicksburg and Gettysburg, and Lincoln was seeking a second term. His old commander, General McCellan, worked to defeat him in the polls. Into this atmosphere, the 1864 General Conference gathered from all across the northern states in Philadelphia. Waiting for them were Issac Hinson and sixteen others. It had been sixteen years since they first presented their case for their own conference within the Methodist Episcopal Church. By now, they had garnered more support among the delegates, like Adam Wallace, Presiding Elder in Snow Hill District.

Wallace, who had come from the world of business, started as an on-the-job itinerant trainee on the southern end of the Delmarva peninsula.[177] His immersion into Black Methodism was immediate as a new minister at Wesley church in Snow Hill, a Black congregation. He soon found himself praying with African Americans in their cabins. As he continued to serve, he observed that Black members had no church building of their own.

> They worshipped with the whites. The gallery was assigned them; they heard the same sermons, spoke in the same love feasts, communed at the same table of the Lord, and were led in class by the same circuit preachers."[178]

---

177 You can read more about this very interesting man in *My Business Was To Fight the Devil*, edited by Joseph F. DiPaolo and on the Barratt's Chapel website (www.barratts.org) under Peninsula Methodist (1885-1887).

178 *Peninsula Methodist Magazine*, March 14, 1885.

This Irish-born Methodist convert, who had experienced first-hand the life of Black Methodists, saw the future Hinson and his colleagues were seeking from the General Conference. He was now the Presiding Elder over the Snow Hill District, which covered the southernmost end of the Delmarva Peninsula from Seaford, Delaware, south to Cape Charles. He had Union, Confederate, and Black members over which he presided. At his quarterly conferences, he offered Black leaders the privilege of voting. When he saw their reluctance to vote for fear of threats to their lives, he started Black-only quarterly conferences to illustrate that these men were capable of leading the most fundamental unit of American Methodism.

Wallace was a man of unusual courage. A number of Confederate sympathizers in his District were so incensed over the issuing of the Emancipation Proclamation that they burned down Black churches. An unexpected act of decency, the arsonists removed the Bibles and hymnals from a church before they lit the torch that reduced the sanctuary to ash.

In response, Wallace took the radical step of getting the approval from the commander to have the Union soldiers of the Maryland Home Guard go to all the Confederate homes within three miles of each burned Black church and collect money to rebuild the churches. He deposited the money in a Seaford, Delaware bank. Black members used the money to rebuild their own churches back to even better than they were before the arson. After the war, with the soldiers discharged, Southern lawyers filed a claim that the people were unjustly taxed and wanted Wallace to repay them. He did repay the widows with the money left over from rebuilding all the churches.[179]

---

179 *Peninsula Methodist Magazine*, April 9, 1887.

With his place among the General Conference delegates, he was the man committed to take up the cause of a new Black annual conference. But other delegates questioned the need for a Black annual conference: Where was the data? Was it worth their time as delegates to approve it and find a bishop's to preside over it? Since the 1860 General Minutes no longer counted Black members, most delegates had no knowledge of how many Blacks were members of their church. The only delegates who had this information were in the Baltimore and Philadelphia Conference Journals, which were not widely distributed. Others questioned if such an act was legal. Underlying their objections was the understanding, if such a conference were approved, Black delegates would join them at the next General Conference as equals.

Wallace and others pushed ahead with the resolution. It was referred to the Committee on the State of the Work among the People of Color.

After deliberating in committee, they delivered to the General Conference the following report:[180]

REPORT NO., I OF THE COMMITTEE ON THE STATE OF THE WORK AMONG THE PEOPLE OF COLOR.

We, a majority of the Committee on the State of the Work among the People of Color, after as careful an examination of the subject as we could well give it from the data at our command, have reached and beg leave to report the following facts and conclusions:

1. Though, owing to the unsettled state of the country, we have no means of ascertaining the exact number of our

---

180 *Proceedings of the General Conference Methodist Episcopal Church 1864*, pages 194, 226

colored members and attendants on the ministrations of our Church, yet from former statistics we are impressed that they are not inconsiderable. The bishops in their address to the General Conference of 1856| stated that in the Border Slave States alone there was a colored membership including probationers, of about 27,000, with the attendants upon our ministry, making a probable population of upward of 100,000. This statement they substantially reaffirmed in their address to the General Conference of 1860. When, with the close of the present rebellion, these scattered sheep shall have been gathered again, we think it probable that an advance upon the above exhibit of numbers will result.

2. The war, in breaking the fetters of oppression everywhere, is appealing another and a larger class to the prompt and efficient missionary enterprise of the Church. That portion of them who have been until recently under the care of the Methodist Episcopal Church, South, will, in the nature of the case, seek a home with some other branch of the Methodist family; all will need religious instruction and ecclesiastical oversight.

3. As a Church we have never sought, do not now seek to ignore our duty to the colored population. A persistent testimony against oppression on our part has been accompanied by earnest effort for the moral and religious improvement of the oppressed. Nor has our labor been in vain in the Lord. Public sentiment owes much of its present high moral tone on the subject of slavery to the testimony we have borne against it, and among no people in proportion to population have we had more seals to our ministry than among the slaves. Deprivation, by circumstances beyond our control, of our appropriate jurisdiction over the extreme Southern slave, has not destroyed our sympathy for him, nor lessened our disposition to welcome him back to our protection.

4. If it be a principle patent to Christian enterprise that the missionary field itself must produce the most efficient missionaries, our colored local preachers are peculiarly important to us at this time. With these properly marshaled, what hindereth that we go down and possess the land?

5. But how can they be properly marshaled ? Shall they be advised to seek a union with some one of the several independent African Methodist Churches of this country under the assurance that the patronage of our Church shall, for the more perfect command of this interesting field, be extended to the union when effected? Or shall they remain as *local preachers* to be employed by the presiding elders where their services may be needed? Or shall the doors of the existing Annual Conferences be thrown open to them? Or shall they be organized into Mission Conferences, with a view to test and develop their adaptation to this peculiar work?

6. In reply to these questions we are somewhat prepared to speak advisedly, having direct information from delegates to the General Conference familiar with this work; from intelligent and trustworthy local preachers who have been deputed by the colored charges in Delaware, Maryland, and the District of Columbia to represent them before the committee; and from various memories setting forth the wishes of our colored members.

From these sources we gather the following facts:

(1) Our colored members, ministers, and laymen feel that the times are auspicious to the development of their mental and moral power, and request from us the facilities necessary to this end.

(2) A colored pastorate they recognize as among the most important of these facilities, securing to them a ministry adapted to their wants, encouraging their young men to enter the ministerial field, and offering motive and opportunity for general ministerial advancement.

(3) They do not, however, propose to secure this by — indeed they are utterly opposed to — separation from our Church, either with a view to a union with another, or to independent organization. With such a feeling on their part the General Conference cannot consistently with its own responsibility, with their constitutional rights, or with any decent recognition of their loyalty to our Church in all the troubles through which, on their account, she has passed, adopt any measure which shall, even indirectly, look to such a result.

(4) Conference organization is asked for from two quarters; other memorials urge that the requests should be granted. The local ministers who have been before us have shown deep solicitude in this direction.

7. From this exhibit of facts two convictions are natural, namely: we must retain the oversight of this people — we must give them efficient colored pastors.

To retain these pastors as mere local preachers, subject to appointment by white presiding elders, will impair rather than increase their efficiency — will promote Congregationalism among them, rather than itinerant missionary enterprise.

To propose their incorporation with the existing Annual Conferences will be attended with difficulties too formidable every way to be readily disposed of, and the delay incident to such a proposition is incompatible with the urgent requirements of the times.

In view of these considerations we recommend to the General Conference for adoption the following:

PREAMBLE AND RESOLUTION

Whereas, In the present circumstances of our country, the colored people occupy a position of peculiar interest, appealing to our Chistian sympathy, and inviting our missionary enterprise; and

Whereas, This enterprise cannot now be made efficient by the policy of our Church hitherto pursued toward them, and special measures have therefore become necessary; and

Whereas, The exigencies of the case require to efficiency prompt action; therefore be it

1. Resolved, By the General Conference of the Methodist Episcopal Church in Conference assembled, that it is the duty of our Church to encourage *colored pastorates for colored people* wherever practicable, and to contribute to their efficiency by every means in our power.

2. Resolved, That the efficiency of said pastorates can be best promoted by distinct conference organizations, and that therefore the bishops be and they are hereby authorized to organize among our colored ministers, for the benefit of our colored members and population, Mission Conferences — one or more — where in their godly judgment the exigencies of the work may demand it; and should more than one be organized, to determine their boundaries until the meeting of the next General Conference, said conference or conferences to possess all the powers usual to Mission Annual Conferences. Provided, that nothing in this

resolution be so construed as to impair the existing constitutional rights of our colored members on the one hand, or to forbid, on the other, the transfer of white ministers to said conference or conferences where it may be practicable and deemed necessary.

3. Resolved, That our General Missionary Committee be requested to take into careful consideration the condition of our colored people, and should conferences be organized among them, make to them—consistently with other demands upon its funds—such appropriations as may be essential to success. Signed for and in behalf of the Committee,

J. McKendree Reiley, Chairman. Adam Wallace, Secretary.

REPORT NO. 2 OF THE COMMITTEE ON THE STATE OF THE WORK AMONG THE PEOPLE OF COLOR.[181]

The following resolution referred first to the Committee on Revisals (act of revising), was, upon the recommendation of said committee, referred by the General Conference to the Committee on the State of the Work among the People of Color, namely:

Resolved, That the Committee on Revisals be instructed to inquire whether there exists in the laws of our Church any obstacle to the reception into the various Annual Conferences of as many colored preachers as will supply the colored Churches established or to be established among us.

We, the Committee to whom this subject was finally referred, beg leave to report that we are not aware of any legal obstacle

---

181 Ibid, pages 226, 253.

to the reception of colored preachers into our Annual Conferences.

J. M'Kendree Reiley, Chairman. Adam Wallace, Secretary.
As he later wrote, "the General Conference of 1864 …after
long debate, adopted the plan I found necessary for their
well-being throughout the Snow Hill District."[182]

Wallace had prevailed. Now, two new Black annual conferences
were to be established: Delaware and Washington. The criterion to
form the new conferences was set at a minimum of ten Elders who
had been under the supervision of a presiding elder for at least two
years. Wallace had asked Bishop Scott for the opportunity to leave
his position and work with the new conference. The Bishop denied
his request because he knew they could make it on their own.

July 1864

Two months after the General Conference's adjournment, Bishop
Edmond S. Janes of New Jersey called the organizing session of the
Delaware Annual Conference to order in the John Wesley Methodist
Episcopal Church in Philadelphia.[183] This was Bishop Janes' twentieth
year as bishop. Like his twin brother, a Methodist pastor in New
Jersey, he knew the people, the area, and the possibilities. He would
later be honored by Blacks naming their congregations after him.

This was a new beginning for Methodism and America. The
Delaware Conference was built upon the pride, dedication, and

---

182 *Peninsula Methodist Magazine*, December 4, 1886. cf Joseph DiPaolo, *My Business
was to Fight the Devil*, Tapestry Press: Acton, MA, 1998, p. 316.

183 "I yesterday met my coloured brothers—some thirty of them. A very pleasant
meeting with them. The coloured (Delaware) Conference of the Methodist Episcopal Church is no humbug (no hoax). It is a grand beginning of good things to the
poor coloured people'" Letter to his twin brother (Henry Bascom Ridgaway, *The
Life of Edmond S Janes*, p. 277).

humility of African-American Methodists. These men had prepared themselves for many years for this moment in Methodist and American history. A few were born in the 18th century and the youngest in 1827. In spite of being too old to serve, many of them had registered for the draft and had sons fighting for the Union. One had been a slave until 1864, while others had been freed earlier through their own payment or were born free. They all had one common goal—their own annual conference. The names of the Delaware Conference founders are as follows:

Issac Hinson (65 years old), the leader in seeking the General Conference to establish a Black annual conference, was born in 1799 in Kent County, Maryland. He was ordained as an Elder in 1857 and served in New Jersey across from Philadelphia.

John G. Manluff (50) was born in 1814 in Milford, Delaware. Ordained an Elder in 1860.

Joshua Brinkley (48), a close associate of Adam Wallace, was born in 1815 in Wilmington, Delaware.

Isaiah Broughton (47) was born in 1817 in Worcester County, Maryland.

James Davis was born in Montgomery County, Maryland, and by 1857, he was ordained Elder. He was elected as the first delegate to the General Conference in 1868.

Samuel Dale (65), born in 1799, was ordained Elder by 1860.

Nathan Young (39), born in 1825 in Ellendale, Delaware, was an ordained Elder by 1860.

Jehu H. Pierce (37), born in 1827, was the youngest member and was ordained an Elder by 1863.

Wilmore S. Elsey (59), born in 1805 in Somerset County, Maryland, was elected Secretary.

Harrison Smith (39) was born in 1825.

Frost Pullet (76), born in 1788 in Princess Anne, Maryland, was the oldest attending and elected President.

David Tilghman (42), born in 1822 in Chestnut Hill, Pennsylvania, was elected treasurer.

Stephen Johns (45), born in 1818 in Dorchester County, had been a slave for less than a year before the conference.

They chose to name their conference Delaware, in spite of it encompassing Virginia's and Maryland's Eastern Shore, Delaware, the Philadelphia and New Jersey areas. The conference was incorporated in the state of Delaware, which may have been one reason for taking that name. Another reason may be to include all the geographic bodies under the name of Delaware, because Delaware was the first state to sign the ratification of the U.S. Constitution. Like the State of Delaware, whose motto is the 'state that started a nation', the Delaware Conference became the first Black conference to take its place among the white and German annual conferences as an equal.

American Methodist Episcopal System
1784–1864

Quarterly Conference
CIRCUIT

- Classes (Small Groups): Black/white

- Meeting Houses (Church Buildings)

- Camp Meetings (August): Black/white
- Love Feasts (Black/white)
- Approved + Dismissed Black/white: Class Leaders, Exhorters, Local Preachers
- Only white laity voted
- Chair: Presiding Elder (white)

Annual Conference

- Approved candidates for ordained ministry: Deacons + Traveling Elders (white)
- Only Traveling Elders voted
- Chair: Bishop

General Conference
(EVERY 4 YEARS)

- Approved Book of Discipline (rules for the church)
- Only delegated Traveling Elders voted
- Chair: Bishop

NOTES

- Traveling Elders ususally served 2 years on a circuit before being sent to a new circuit
- All meetings of quarterly, annual, and genreal conferences rotated to a new place for each meeting

American Methodist Episcopal System
1864–1939

Quarterly Conference
CIRCUIT

- All functions of local ministry are to whites
- Whites voted
- Chair: Presiding Elder (white)

Quarterly Conference
CIRCUIT

- All functions of local ministry are to Blacks
- Blacks voted
- Chair: Presiding Elder (Black)

Philadelphia Annual Conference

- Determined ordination of white clergy
- Traveling Elders (white) voted
- Chair: Bishop (white)

Delaware Annual Conference

- Determined ordination of Black clergy
- Traveling Elders (Black) voted
- Chair: Bishop (white)

Council of Bishops: white 1784–1920

General Conference
(EVERY 4 YEARS)

- Approved Book of Discipline (rules for the church)
- Only delegated Traveling Elders (Black/white) voted
- Chair: Bishop (white)

NOTES

- Blacks gained control of their local ministry; ordained their own clergy; and voted at General Conference
- First Black bishop elected in 1920 for Black Annual Conferences

The two graphs above outline the major structural change for Blacks within the dominant white Methodist Episcopal Church in the North.

1. Instead of being under the control of a white led quarterly (size of a county or smaller) conference, they controlled all their ministries in the Delaware Conference from New Jersey to the Eastern Shore of Virginia.

2. Instead of white controlled quarterly conferences determining who will be their local preachers and ordained clergy, they now elect their own lay preachers and ordain their clergy. This entitled Black clergy for the first time to hold the status of a Traveling Elder and be appointed as a Presiding Elder over a quarterly conference.

3. Before Black members had no representation at General Conference. Now each of the annual conferences would elect and send delegates with a voice and a vote. The all-white quadrennial gathering ended.

4. At that time, bishops were elected at the General Conference. Now, their delegates could advocate for electing Black bishops.

5. Having their own annual conference gave them the same status as a white annual conference.

A few months later, the second Black conference to form took the name of the country's capital, Washington. Patriotism has always been an American value for Black people. Ponder for a moment how many African Americans proudly carry the name 'Washington.' The Delaware and Washington Annual Conferences have now positioned their Black members to be able to fully function in every aspect of the church, except bishop. This barrier was not in the church law but prejudice.

In 1868, the Delaware[184] and Washington conferences sent the first duly elected delegates to the General Conference meeting in Chicago. The Delaware Conference elected James Davis over Wilmore S. Elsey by a vote of 17-6 to be the first Black delegate to the General Conference. Rev. Elsey served as a Reserve Delegate. The Washington Conference elected Benjamin Brown as its delegate and John P. Bowser, Reserve Delegate. The Blacks of the southernmost end of the northern Methodist Episcopal Church had found 'A Way Out of No Way.'

Nowhere else in America did Blacks have an uninterrupted place at the table in a predominately white organization. They did so briefly in the U.S. Congress during Reconstruction. That ended in 1879 with Joseph Rainey's electoral defeat. It would be 1942 with William Dawson's election before a Black person again took a seat in the U.S. House of Representatives. In the U.S. Senate, Blanche K. Bruce was the only Black elected and served a full term from 1875-1881. The next Black Senator to serve a full term was in 1967 when Edward Brooke was sworn into office.

In contrast to Congress, all subsequent Methodist General Conferences have had Black delegates to this day. Their goal of having a Black bishop in America was petitioned in 1876. Like the founding of

---

184 The secretary described Delaware Conference: shall include the Territory _north and west of the Washington Conference_ and east of the summit of the Alleghany mountains. Delaware is east of Washington to the Atlantic Ocean!

an equal Black conference, a Black bishop equal to a white bishop was put off until 1920 with the election of Robert Elijah Jones. Not until 1964 did an African-American bishop preside over a white annual conference — 100 years after the first Black annual conference was organized.

1965

As the roadblocks were removed for Blacks to be elected bishops and serve in all annual conferences, the movement for integration was moving forward with lightning speed within The Methodist Church (the 1939 union of three denominations). The manner in which integration proceeded can be summarized by what James Baldwin said on December 10, 1986, at the National Press Club, twenty-one years after 1965:

> White people think I am the problem. I'm not the problem. Your history is the problem. You can't liberate me. You can't liberate yourselves. We are in this together. Your answer is to make me white. I want to grow up, and you should too.

The struggle to establish the Delaware Conference, which took sixteen years from 1848 to 1864, took only three years to be eliminated in 1965. In Baldwin's words, Black annual conferences, like Delaware, were the problem and needed to be divided and swallowed up by five white annual conferences. It was not even discussed whether white conferences needed to change their conference boundaries.[185] The old prejudice of not seeing Blacks as equals was still alive. The ultimate consequence after one hundred and one years of being equal was that history returned her members to being the few among the many—a return to the year 1848. The equalization of pensions for Black clergy with whites and higher salaries was a notable achievement financially. It still did not change the enlightened attitudes of white Methodist leaders who saw the presence of Blacks having their own conference as the problem, instead of their achievement of being the first to become equal.

---

185 Author's conversation with the leader of the merger movement.

CHAPTER 17

African Americans: Shattering and Regathering

Toward the end of his life, Bishop Asbury focused on the development of northern African Methodism. He may not have imagined how many Africans would become southern Methodists by the time of the Civil War. Southern African Methodism had grown to where it dwarfed its northern counterpart's membership. These southern Blacks became the prize for northern Methodist church denominations to seek to make their own out of the shambles of war. An intense struggle ensued among the African and the white northern Methodists on who could enlist the largest number of Southern African Methodists, as Lucius Holsey explained:

> After I received the appointment, I . . . went to Savannah to take charge of the colored church known as 'Andrew Chapel.' But this church was seized upon by the African Methodist Episcopal Connection and was then in litigation. As there was no way for me to get or use the church, the white people of Trinity church in Savannah gave me their library to preach in.[186]

---

186 Lucius Henry Holsey, *Autobiography* reprint (Atlanta: The Franklin Printing Co, 1898), 23.

Bishop Lakey writes in "The History of the CME Church":

Upon hearing that the African Methodist Episcopal bishops were petitioning the 1866 General Conference of the Methodist Episcopal Church, South, for a relationship with that church for the colored members, (Isaac) Lane and others responded vociferously: 'At once – we made it known that we preferred a separate organization of our own, regularly established after our ideas and notions.

. . . These leaders (Methodist Episcopal Church, South), though somewhat taken back and quite offended by the withdrawal of so many of their colored members, nevertheless recognized that they had to deal with thousands of former slave members who, neither persuaded by the appeals of the African Methodist Episcopal and African Methodist Episcopal Zion churches nor tempted by the opportunities offered by the Methodist Episcopal Church (white), were looking to them for religious guidance.[187]

Accordingly, Holland N. McTyeire observed

"The remnant that clave (to the Methodist Episcopal Church, South) at their request were constituted an independent body under a name chosen by themselves."[188]

To grasp the scope and swiftness of the realignments between these four Methodist denominations, let us look at the numbers: The first graph is 1815, the year before the African Methodist

---

187 Lakey, *The History of the CME Church* (Nashville: Parthenon Press, 1985), 116-117, 128. Rev. Isaac Lane was ordained deacon in 1866; an elder in 1867; and appointed presiding elder of the Jackson District of the Memphis Colored Conference.
188 McTyeire, p. 385

1815

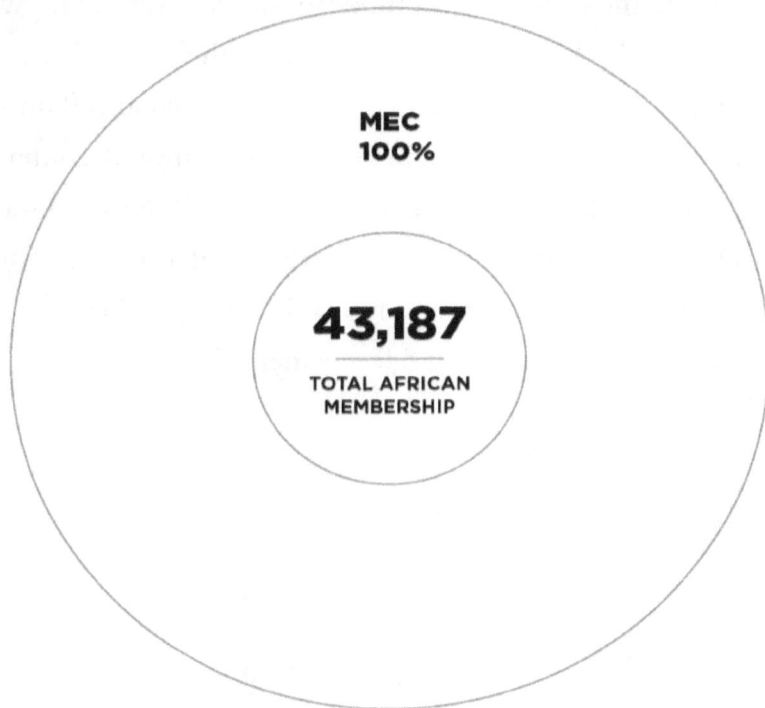

MEC
100%

43,187

TOTAL AFRICAN
MEMBERSHIP

MEC - Methodist Episcopal Church

Episcopal Church was established and all African American Methodists were still in the Methodist Episcopal Church.[189]

This second graph shows the effects of the 1844 division and the outreach work the Southern Methodist Church engaged in, where most Black Methodists were in 1860 before the start of the Civil War. Though annual conferences, like Philadelphia and Baltimore, counted African American members in their annual conference reports, the northern Methodist Episcopal Church's General Minutes no longer had a line listing its Black membership. For our purposes, the Spencer churches are not listed since they remained in the mid-Atlantic area and had fewer members.

---

189 *Minutes of Methodist Episcopal Church,* 1815.

1860 (Before Civil War)

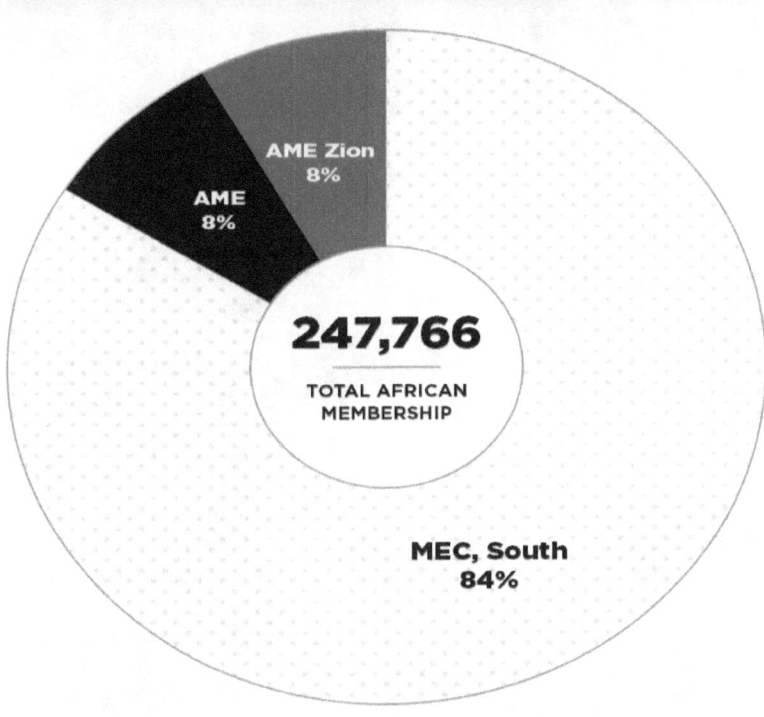

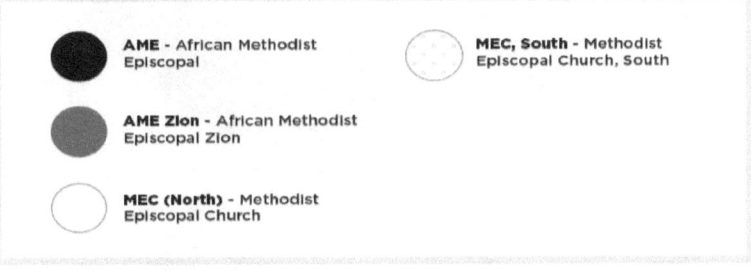

The third graph [1870] shows the dramatic reshuffling of African-American Methodism in the last ten years.

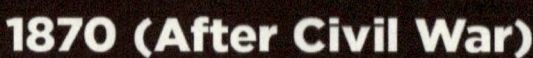

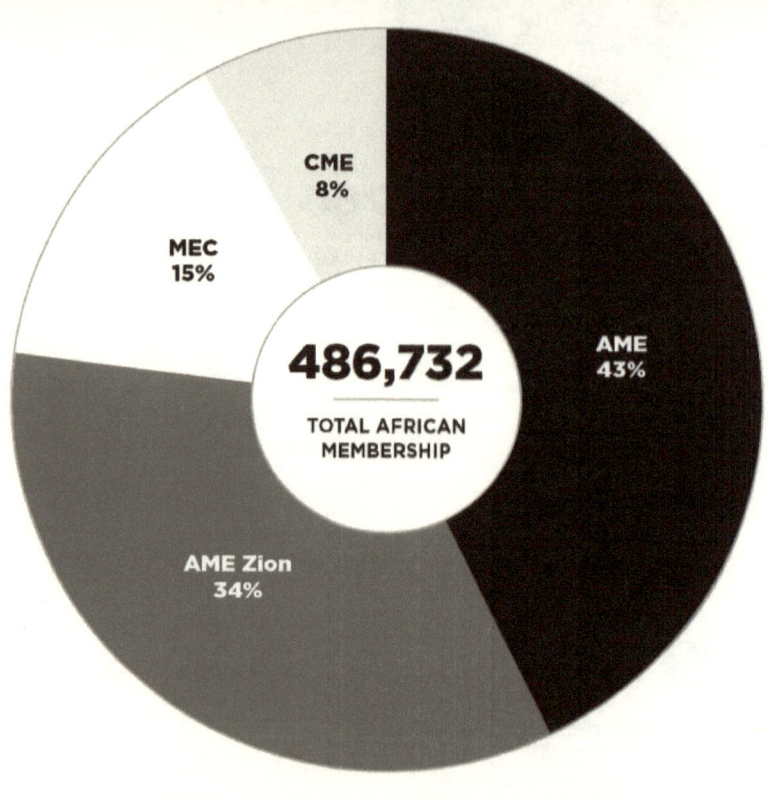

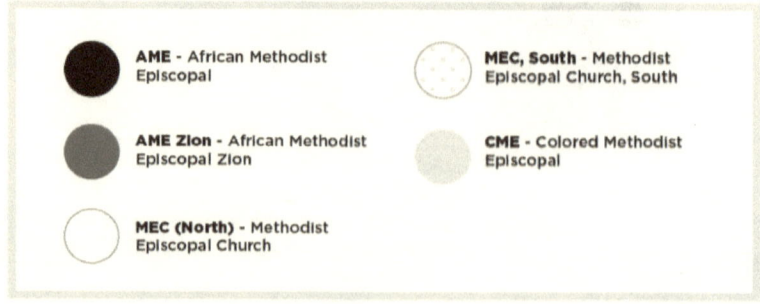

For the first time, the African Methodist Episcopal Church had the largest African membership, and the Methodist Episcopal Church, South, no longer had any Blacks as members. The African Methodist Episcopal Zion Church had the second largest membership,[190] while the northern Methodist Episcopal Church was in third position.

The southern African Methodists who refused to join the northern denominations — Black and white — became the only African church controlled by Southerners living in the South. The name they chose for themselves was the "Colored Methodist Episcopal Church."[191]

There was a failed attempt in 1920 to merge all three Black Methodist denominations and call themselves the 'United Methodist Episcopal Church.' In recent years, the Christian MEC and AME Zion have had ongoing attempts to merge the two denominations to no avail. In America, "united" is a tricky word!

The consequence of the Civil War for Black Methodists now allowed each person to self-select which Methodist church one chose to be a member anywhere in the United States; whereas, white Methodists were still divided between north and south until 1939.

To join in the 'What Ifs' of history: At the end of the Civil War, there existed in the South a near equal number of African and white Methodists.[192] If they could have become one church, where one did not control the other, would America have seen a 'new birth

---

190 www.Wikipedia. African Methodist Episcopal Zion Church quotes *Annual Cyclopedia* 1866, page 492.

191 In 1954, the Colored Methodist Episcopal Church changed 'Colored' in its name to 'Christian' to let people know all races were welcome as members.

192 All of the Southern African American Methodists by 1870 would have represented an adult membership of more than 513,889, and the white Southern Methodist Church had 540,80 members. That would have been a church of over 1 million members with a racial balance never seen in America.

of freedom' where 'all men are created equal' within the Southern Methodist Church?

Since that did not happen, the question still hangs in the air: Would there ever come a day in Methodism where there would be an annual conference with an equal number of Black and white members? There was an opportunity in The Methodist Church when Black and white conferences merged to remove 'segregated' structures from 1965 onward. The result was the opposite. Black annual conferences paid the price in the loss of control, identity, and were reduced to small parts and fitted into much larger white annual conferences. What had been created as equals in 1864 was returned to the status of 1848. This was not by reactionary racists but by liberal, progressive Methodists, who lost no control or power over their affairs. In our own time, The United Methodist Church continues to create larger annual conferences through mergers that continue the trend of reducing the voice and experience of her African-American members.

To summarize our story, African-American Methodists have chosen to express themselves through five different denominations and yet all of them call themselves Methodists. The catalytic experience in the creation of a Methodist identity for enslaved men and women goes back to the man who did more to fulfill their aspirations — Francis Asbury, when he was introduced to American (not British) African Methodists in Philadelphia in 1771.

CHAPTER 18

The London Conference

The first global gathering of Methodists convened at Wesley's Chapel on London's City Road on Wednesday, September 7, 1881. This was eleven years after the last branch of African American Methodism, Colored [Christian] Methodist Episcopal Church, was formed from the remaining Black members of Southern Methodism.

Bishop McTyerie, a former missionary to the southern slaves and now bishop, ordained and consecrated the first bishops of the Colored Methodist Episcopal Church. He reflected on the history of African Methodism:

When (Bishop Thomas) Coke landed on the continent, Black Harry, unable to read, was the most advanced specimen of African Christianity he met with. On the general emancipation, affected by the Civil War, Southern Methodism showed thousands of negro preachers, exhorters, and class—leaders, who could read their Bible and edify their congregations. . . And when the sons of Wesley, from all parts of the world, gathered at City Road Chapel in Ecumenical Conference, African bishops were there as representative members, who had never seen Africa.[193]

The global conference was the brainchild of the Methodist Episcopal Church meeting in Baltimore on May 31, 1876. The delegates gave the bishops authority to form a special committee to seek out the willingness of other Methodist churches to meet as an Ecumenical Conference. From thirty Methodist churches came four hundred delegates from around the world to City Road, London, the site of Wesley Chapel and the grave of John Wesley. As the delegates streamed into the Chapel and took their seats, few had ever seen each other face to face. Before their eyes, they glimpsed the breadth of the Wesleyan movement from its humble beginnings in England. The conference had a profound effect on her African American delegates. William Walls wrote:

> The conference …exhibited deep Christian courtesy as far as black church leadership was concerned. Bishop L.H. Holsey of CME Church, Bishop J.P. Thompson and Rev. J. McHenry Farley of AME Zion Church and Bishop Daniel A. Payne of the AME Church were invited speakers, and Bishop Payne assisted in administering the Lord's Supper and served as one of the secretaries of the conference. Other black church leaders became active participants in the discussions and debates. Bishop J.W. Hood (AME Zion) made a striking plea for unity in Home mission efforts, and the noted Dr. J. C. Price won his fame as a "world orator" in his eloquent responses and general remarks on vital issues brought forth for the betterment of Methodism. Dr. Price particularly stressed education

---

193 McTyerie, page 385.

and mission for blacks in Africa and America. Dr. Price remained in Great Britain for a year, lecturing and raising the funds that established Livingston College.[194]

To grasp the breadth of competent leadership that had been developed among African American Methodists, below is a summary of each one who made presentations and served on the committee:

From African Methodist Episcopal Bishop Daniel A. Payne serving on the planning committee, Black Americans were involved in formal addresses throughout the conference:

Second Day, Thursday, September 8th. Rev. Bishop L. H. Holsey, Colored Methodist Episcopal Church of America, gave an address—*Methodism: Its History and Results.*[195]

Fourth Day, Saturday, September 10th. Rev. J. McHenry Farley, Methodist Episcopal Zion Church, the address: *Methodism and the Young.*[196]

Fifth Day, Monday, September 12th. Rev. Bishop D. A. Payne, African Methodist Episcopal Church, *The Lord's Day and Temperance and on Relation of Methodism to the Temperance Movement.*[197]

Sixth Day, Tuesday, September 13th. Rev. Bishop J. P. Thompson, Methodist Episcopal Zion Church, *Possible Perils of Methodism and From Innovations upon Established Methodist Usages and Institutions.*[198]

Seventh Day, Wednesday, September 14th. Bishop L. H. Holsey, Colored Methodist Episcopal Church of America,

---

194 Walls, page 478.
195 *Proceedings* London, pages 41-97.
196 Ibid, pages 156-188.
197 Ibid, pages 189-246.
198 Ibid, pages 247-300.

presented a resolution relating to the publication of a Catechism.[199]

On the **Twelfth Day, Tuesday, September 20th,** Prof. J. P. Shorter, African Methodist Episcopal Church, on the subject: *Christian Unity and the Catholicity of Methodism.*[200]

Below is the list of the invited African-American representatives. It gives us a glimpse of the progress African-Americans had made within American society since slavery ended.

From the **Methodist Episcopal Church:**[201]

Rev. Edward W. S. Peck, Washington, DC. Pastoral record: 1878-1881, pastor Asbury in DC.; 1882-1884 Presiding Elder; 1891 - Pastor John Wesley. At the time of the conference, he was a Presiding Elder in the Washington Conference.

Rev. Peck was the only African-American in the MEC delegation; however, it included the noted Union Civil War General Clinton B. Fisk of Seabright, New Jersey, who had secured a site to house the Fisk College in a former military barracks with a $30,000 gift for its endowment. At that time, Fisk was assistant commissioner of the Freedmen's Bureau of Tennessee. His gift created educational opportunities for generations of young Black people, like the late Representative John Lewis of Georgia.

From the **African Methodist Episcopal Church.**[202] Of the four bishops invited, three were able to attend.

Bishop Daniel Alexander Payne, D.D., was born in Charleston, S.C., on February 24, 1811. He was elected as the sixth Bishop in 1852. The degree of Doctor of Divinity was conferred on him by Wilberforce University, of which he later became its president, the first Black college

---

199 Ibid, page 301.
200 Ibid, pages 551-604.
201 Ibid.
202 Ibid.

president in the USA and visited Europe in 1867. At the Ecumenical Council, he presided one day over the deliberations to the satisfaction of all present.

Bishop John Mifflin Brown, D.D., L.C.D., was born on September 8, 1817, in Odessa (then called Cantwell's Bridge), Delaware. His grandfather was a Methodist Episcopal local preacher. In January 1836, he joined Bethel AME church in Philadelphia and became an important activist in the Underground Railroad. Ordained a Deacon, September 1846; later an Elder; and consecrated as the 11th Bishop in May 1868. Following the Civil War, on July 25, 1868, he organized the Alabama Conference in Selma, Alabama. He died on March 16, 1893.

Bishop James Alexander Shorter. Wilberforce, Ohio. Born in Washington, DC, on February 4, 1817. He entered the itinerant ministry in April 1846 in Ohio. In 1868, He was elected as the 9th Bishop and sent to organize the church in the extreme Southwest, Arkansas, Louisiana, and Texas. After the London Conference, he traveled to France and Switzerland. As president of the missionary society, he succeeded in opening the work in Haiti and Africa.

Bishop William F. Dickerson, D.D. Born in 1845, he was elected in 1880 at the age of 36, the 13th and youngest Bishop of the AME Church. Developed the AME Church in South Carolina and Georgia. At the London Conference, he served on the Business Committee. Tragically, he died four years later.

Rev. Benjamin Franklin Lee, D.D. Wilberforce, Ohio. He was born September 18, 1841, in Bridgeton, NJ. At Wilberforce University, he became a full student in 1865, graduating with an A. B. degree in 1872. He received support from Hannah McDonald, a sister-in-law to Bishop Daniel Payne, who was the university's president. Licensed to preach in 1868; ordained deacon in 1870; Elder in 1872; and elected Bishop in 1892. He returned to Wilberforce in 1876, taking the position of University president upon the resignation of Bishop Payne. He held the position for eight years, and in 1884, he resigned to take the position of editor of the AME Church's official paper, the *Christian Recorder.* He died in 1926.

Rev. James Matthew Townsend. Richmond, Indiana. He lived from 1841 to 1913. A Civil War soldier in 54 Massachusetts Colored Infantry. Service as a school principal and as Missionary Secretary, 1878-1885, he traveled abroad. State Legislator. Pastor

Rev. Augustus T. Case [203]. Charlestown, South Carolina. He was born in December 1806, a slave, and purchased his freedom for himself and his family. Before the Civil War, he ran a livery stable. The MEC, South, licensed him to preach. After the War, he and his followers— some estimates put it at 3,000—joined the AMEC. He became a Presiding Elder over the Edisto District of the South Carolina Conference. He died on August 6, 1881.

Rev. James Crawford Embry from Leavenworth, Kansas, lived from 1834 to 1897. In the Civil War, he served on a supply boat carrying provisions for the Army under General Grant. In 1869, he was elected as the 25th Bishop. He was the Financial Secretary of AMEC (1879-1884) and, in 1884, elected Business Manager of the Publication Department.

Alexander Clark, Esq. Iowa City, Iowa. Lived from 1826 to 1891. He helped recruit soldiers for Iowa's 60th Colored Troops in the Civil War. At age 37, he enlisted but did not muster because of an infirmity in his foot. In 1868, he sued to have his daughter go to a better and closer white school. He won the case, and it was referred to in the *Brown* v. *Board of Education* case before the US Supreme Court. In 1881, he was

---

203　Handy, *Scraps of AME History,* page 267.

an investor in the Chicago newspaper, *The Conservator*, and later was its owner. From 1890-1891, he was the US Ambassador to Liberia.

Prof. Joseph P. Shorter, A.M. Wilberforce, Ohio, was a Teacher at Wilberforce College.

Mr. Nelson T. Gant, Zanesville, Ohio, lived from 1821 to 1905. He sought and won in 1845/6 for the first time to have his slave marriage determined in court to be legal in Virginia. He was a former slave conductor on the Underground Railroad. Once free, he moved to Zanesville, where he owned and farmed 300 acres, a saltlick, and a coal mine. His house today is open to the public.

Joseph W. Morris, Esq. Cokesbury, South Carolina, lived from 1850 to 1913. Born free, he graduated from Howard University in 1875. Afterward, he enrolled in South Carolina University Law School and passed the bar Exam in 1876. He became a principal of Payne Institute, which merged into Allen University. In 1885, he became its president.

African Methodist Episcopal Zion Church[204] Four bishops were invited, and three attended.

Bishop James Walker Hood of Fayetteville, North Carolina, was born in Kennett Township, Chester County, Pennsylvania, on May 30, 1831; ordained Deacon September 2, 1860; Elder June 15, 1862; and consecrated 17th Bishop on July 3, 1872. At the end of the Civil War, he was sent as one of the first missionaries to North Carolina. Having served 44 active years as Bishop, he retired in 1916 and died on October 30, 1918.[205]

Bishop Singleton Thomas Webster Jones, D.D. of Washington, D. C. was born in Wrightsville, York County, PA, on March 8, 182 and ordained Deacon on August 12, 1850; Elder on August 15, 1851; and

---

204 Ibid.
205 Walls, page 578.

consecrated on May 31, 1868, as the 16th Bishop. He was a founder and editor of *Zion's Standard and Weekly Review.* He served as bishop for 23 years and died on April 18, 1891.[206]

Bishop William Henry Hillery of Pittsburg, Pennsylvania, was born in Virginia in May 1839 and moved to Wilkes-Barre, PA. He was ordained Deacon on November 10, 1864; Elder on November 16, 1866; and consecrated the 19th Bishop on July 4, 1876. He was 'disrobed' on May 12, 1884, and died on July 22, 1893.[207]

Bishop Joseph Pascal Thompson, M.D. D.D. of Newburg, New York, was born into slavery on December 20, 1818, at Winchester, Virginia. As a youth, he ran away to Pennsylvania, where he studied and practiced medicine in Newburgh, NY. He was part of the Underground Railroad, under the direction of Rev. Dr. Mills of Auburn Seminary, Auburn, NY. He read theology and was ordained Deacon on May 17, 1846; Elder on May 2, 1847; and consecrated as the 18th Bishop on July 4, 1876. He died on December 21, 1894.[208]

Rev. John Bryan Small. A.M. D.D. was born at Frazer, St. Joseph's Parish. Barbados, British West Indies, on March 14, 1845. At St. John's Lodge and at Codrington, he graduated at the head of his class. While traveling in the United States, he joined AME Zion Church and was ordained Deacon on May 26, 1872; Elder on June 1, 1873, and consecrated the 27th Bishop on May 21, 1896. He was the First Bishop to travel to Africa and made Africa part of his District (episcopal area). He died on January 15, 1905, in York, PA.[209]

Prof. William Howard Day of Harrisburg, Pennsylvania, was born in New York City on October 16, 1825. He was baptized by James Varick at Zion Church NY, who shared meals in his family's home. He

206 Ibid, page 577.
207 Ibid, page 579.
208 Ibid, page 578.
209 Ibid, page 586.

was ordained Deacon and Elder in 1866. In 1847, he was the first Black to graduate from Oberlin College. He became an outstanding educator and a close associate of Frederick Douglass. He was the only Black on the Harrisburg School Board. He died on March 13, 1901.

Rev. J. McHenry Farley was born in 1831 in Petersburg, Virginia. From 1871-1873, served as Principal Keeper at New Point Comfort Lighthouse, VA. In 1882, he served as editor of *THE STAR OF ZION*, which enabled him to be deeply involved in many aspects of the church's development.

Rev. Joseph Charles Price of North Carolina. Bishop Hood supported him through Shaw and Lincoln Universities. He was licensed to preach in 1876; ordained Deacon and Elder by Bishop Hood. He was 27 years old when he went to the London Conference and stayed in England for a year, and raised $10,000 for Livingston College. Described as 'the world's orator,' he addressed the Centennial Celebration of the Methodist Christmas Conference held at Lovely Lane, Baltimore, in 1884.

Rev. Samuel Wilson of Mobile, Alabama, was a Southern conference leader.

Rev. Wilbur Garrison Strong of Mobile, Alabama, was born in Hartford, CT. He had served as a school principal before the Civil War. With Emancipation in 1863 and being an ordained Elder, he left New York City on September 26, 1865, for Florida, where he organized conferences in Florida, Alabama, and Louisiana from his base of operations in Mobile.

Coloured Methodist Episcopal Church Of America.[210] Six people were invited, but only one Bishop was able to attend the conference.

Bishop Lucius Henry Holsey of Augusta, Georgia, was born in slavery on July 3, 1842, in Georgia. His father was James Holsey, who owned the plantation. He taught himself to read and write and gained his freedom when slavery was abolished. He attended the 1870 organizing General Conference of CMEC. He was elected the fourth Bishop in 1873and died on August 3, 1920. "He said of his mother, Louisa, was of 'pure African descent' and his grandfather, Alex, was 'an African of the Africans'."

Rev. C. Wesley Fitzhugh of Virginia was elected Editor of the Book Committee by the 1878 CMEC General Conference.

Rev. H. H. Mitchell of the North Mississippi Conference.

Mr. Lewis Carnish of Washington, D.C.

Mr. Peter Pastell of Hopkinsville, Kentucky, was elected to the Book Committee by the 1878 CMEC General Conference.

Mr. James H. Harper of Augusta, Georgia, was a professor at Lane College.

Each one could be listed in an 'African Methodist Hall of Fame', as representatives of the many who applied their gifts and talents to build a unique Methodism larger than themselves.

CHAPTER 19

The Story of the Reverend Mr. Solomon Jackson

S olomon Jackson took his seat at the third Quarterly Conference meeting in St. Michaels, Talbot County, Maryland. It was Saturday, January 25, 1840.[211] The day is significant for it continued what Jesse Lee had written in 1773: "Quarterly meetings moved from Tuesday to Saturday and Sunday . . . One weighty reason was that many of the slaves could not attend these meetings except on the Lord's Day."[212] Sixty-seven years later, the practice was still being observed.

It was a short journey by boat from Solomon's home church, Waugh Chapel, in Cambridge, Maryland. The Presiding Elder of the Talbot Circuit of the Methodist Episcopal Church was the Reverend David Dailey, who had earlier in his ministry served Solomon's church and the Cambridge community.

---

211 Talbot Quarterly Conference Minutes, January 1840.
212 Jesse Lee, *History of Methodism in America (1807)*, 1773.

Alongside him was the secretary, William Townsend. They were joined by the two pastors who oversaw Methodist classes and officiated at the Sacraments of Baptism and Holy Communion. The room was filled with Talbot County (Bay Hundred) circuit leaders: thirty white and six Black exhorters. The Quarterly Conference had earlier approved each exhorter, because each had demonstrated their exemplary Christian character and possessed the talent for public speaking. No longer practiced today, their role was to exhort the hearers of the sermon to go and do what the preacher had proclaimed. This was the first official step in becoming a local Methodist preacher.

When Presiding Elder Dailey began going through the established agenda, he asked if any lingering character issues were being appealed to the body for action. There were none. The second agenda item was similar to the first: were there any new character issues? There were none.

To illustrate how seriously these Methodists took matters of discipline, it later expelled long-time member Edward Covey, despite his being active for many years in Methodist activities and a man of means. Covey is well-known in the life of Frederick Douglass, who was the slave tamer who tried unsuccessfully to beat Douglass down to submission.

It had been sixteen months since Douglass had escaped from the slavery of his St. Michaels owner, Thomas Auld. As Solomon sat quietly, his eye caught the eye of Thomas Auld, the steward in charge of finances. As Auld looked at Solomon, did his presence recall the gifted and determined slave he had lost to freedom?

Despite Douglass' protestations in his anti-slavery pamphlets criticizing religion, Douglass became a Methodist preacher in the African Methodist Episcopal Zion Church. As tensions mounted in the 1850s, the former St. Michael's pastor, John Long, met in 1857 with Auld's daughter, Amanda, and Douglass for dinner in Philadelphia. On Thomas Auld's deathbed in 1877, he and Douglass had a tearful reunion where Auld told him, "Frederick, I always knew you were too smart to be a slave, and had I been in your place, I should have done as you did."[213]

After the Civil War, the two Black Methodist congregations in Easton – Asbury and Bethel – had Douglass preach the dedicatory sermons in 1878.[214] Though slavery no longer bound Douglass to Talbot County, its Methodism was always present in his life.[215]

Now, Presiding Elder Dailey came to the business of Solomon's presence. The number of Black Methodists had grown to over five hundred, and the Quarterly Conference had not approved a Black Local Preacher. Was that why Solomon was present that Saturday? Had he been invited by Rev. Dailey, who knew him and was aware that the Talbot Quarterly Conference would never approve a Black man to be a Local Preacher? Or, did he come on his own?

Whatever the circumstances of Solomon's presence, he stood before the quarterly conference and requested permission to serve them. To prove he was capable, he presented a certificate of his

---

213 Erin Blakemore, *Frederick Douglass's Emotional Meeting With the Man Who Enslaved Him.* www.history.com.

214 www.frederickdouglassbirthplace.org.

215 Ibid.

credentials as a Licensed Local Preacher, signed by the Presiding Elder
of the Cambridge Circuit, Rev. James A. Massey. The record does not
show if there was any discussion about the advisability of his preaching
there. It only showed their approval in allowing him to serve the African
Americans among them.

As we think of this meeting, it makes us aware of the unique social
situation Methodism had created for Black people. How many Blacks
in 1840 could come before a meeting of whites and have the same
status as a white Licensed Local Preacher? This equality of status is
probably what Solomon appreciated about being a Methodist. The
status it bestowed was a respect for his ability. For all the jerks and twists
over slavery, the Methodist Episcopal Church countered a culture of
racial victimization by bestowing status on enslaved and free African
peoples.

Twenty-four years later, momentous societal changes were
sweeping through the world of Methodism following the Civil War.
African-American Methodists on the Delmarva Peninsula remained by
an accident of geography in the Methodist Episcopal Church after the
1844 division of North and South Methodists. With each Union
victory, the demise of slavery was evident to all Americans. Black
Methodists, like Solomon, had been clamoring for their own annual
conference within the Methodist Episcopal Church.

Finally, the General Conference gave its approval for the first
African-American Annual Conference in the Methodist Episcopal
Church. Bishop Edmund S. Janes called the organizing meeting of the
Delaware Annual Conference to order on Thursday, July 28, 1864.

Instead of Blacks being a few among the many whites, the room was filled with African-American elders, deacons, local preachers, and laity, with only a few white people, like Thomas W. Price. He presented a book on which the official minutes could be recorded for future generations to read about what they had started in Philadelphia. The site of this meeting, Zoar United Methodist Church, has custody of that book.

Each one present that day understood their annual conference stood equal to any white conference or any other African-American denomination. The members of their conference would decide who would be ordained and who would be denied that privilege. The bishop would appoint the presiding elders from their ranks, who in turn would advise the bishop on which pastor needed to be appointed to a particular circuit. They would elect their own delegates to the General Conference, just like the white Methodists. The bishop would be white, but he was the same bishop who presided over the white conference, too—a symbol of unity for Methodists at that time.

The most important business of an annual conference is the election and ordination of the laity into the ordained ministry. Bishop Janes called for the recommendations of local deacons to be ordained as elder to be presented. Solomon Jackson's name was read. He stood before the conference and was elected to be ordained an elder. What emotions must he have experienced? He may have lifted up his hands and shouted, as Methodists did when overcome by the Spirit. Tears must have flowed down his cheeks. His certificate now read: The Reverend Mr. Solomon Jackson, Ordained Elder, Methodist Episcopal Church.

The conference ended the next day. Bishop Janes addressed the body, reminding everyone of the importance of what they had created that summer. The doxology was sung and the bishop called Rev. Solomon Jackson to dismiss the Delaware Conference in prayer. With his spirit full, he prayed fervently for God to bless this new conference. Everyone returned home to their churches and families to continue a Methodist Episcopal ministry that began eighty years ago in Baltimore.

POSTLUDE

Black Methodism Today

The African Methodist Episcopal Church and Bishop Richard Allen are synonymous with the earliest days of African-American Christianity in America. The A.M.E. Church is the largest African American Church in the United States. Its members, clergy, and bishops cover the whole country and are deeply involved in Africa and other parts of the world. With its global reach, 2.5 million members, and 20 active bishops,[216] the AMEC occupies a prominent role in American life.

Four other bodies of the same tradition have a distinctive place within American Christianity. Second in size is the African Methodist Episcopal Zion Church, which began in New York City and now has a membership of 1.4 million.[217] Under the oversight of its eleven bishops, its mission extends throughout the United States to the Caribbean, South America, and Africa.

---

216 African Methodist Episcopal Church. Wikipedia
217 African Methodist Episcopal Zion church. Wikipedia.

The Christian Methodist Episcopal Church is the third largest body with origins in the post-Civil War South. It has a membership of 1.2 million members with eleven bishops in the United States, Haiti, Jamaica, and fourteen African nations.[218]

The fourth body is The United Methodist Church with 319,074 African-American members[219] in 2,400 churches. Blacks are represented at all levels of the church structure. Its first African-American bishop for the United States was elected in 1920. Black bishops are now present in all five American jurisdictions; however, their largest Black membership is in Africa where there are only Black annual conferences..

The fifth Methodist body was founded in 1813 by the Rev. Peter Spencer in Wilmington, Delaware. It is the oldest independent African-American church in the United States. Its original name was the Union Church of Africans. Today, these "Spencer churches" are known as the African Union Methodist Protestant Church and the Union American Methodist Episcopal Church. The fifty-three churches under five episcopal bishops have ministries from Rhode Island to Maryland and in Liberia, West Africa.

These Methodist churches and branches all share one common ancestor: the Methodist Episcopal Church, whose first bishop, Francis Asbury, ordained the first African clergy in America.

---

218 www.cmechurch.org.facts
219 UMDATA. 2024

ACKNOWLEDGMENTS

First, I want to acknowledge the unnamed Africans who arrived on the American shores and their North American descendants. They brought their creative gifts and formed a unique American religious phenomenon—African Methodism. Like the diversity of their African ancestry, this Methodism has expressed itself in a variety of institutional forms, enriching American life to this day.

To help tell this story, I want to thank Mr. Anthony Johnson, Rev. Earle Baker, Rev. Dr. Phil Lawton, Mrs. Connie Connelly, and Ms. Alice Heiserman. Most of all, I want to thank my wife for her loving patience over these many years and her constant admonition: "Make it readable!"

To the blessed memory of my first Counseling Elder, the Rev. Dr. W. Hayward Greene, the epitome of a great African-American Methodist, for guiding me in my first days of pastoral ministry and his passion for Delaware Conference history. His witness is missed.

The mistakes in this manuscript are my creation. As a parishioner often told me: "I may not be right, but I'm never in doubt."

Gary L. Moore
Christmas 2025
Easton, Maryland

APPENDICES

The Early African Methodists on Delaware-Maryland's Eastern Shore.

This partial list is of early African Methodist leaders from the Delaware and Eastern Shore of Maryland, known as the Garden of Methodism, who exercised leadership during the time of slavery and deep racism in American society. This illustrates the impact the Methodist Episcopal Church had on the lives of free and enslaved Africans.

Richard Allen - born (1760) near Dover, Delaware (possibly Philadelphia), into slavery, who did not know his father. Bought his freedom in 1783. Around 1783: Licensed to Preach. Ordained Deacon 1799. Left MEC in 1816 to become the first AMEC Bishop

Joseph Pennington - born (1768 in Queen Anne's County, Maryland, into slavery. Owned by the Ruth family. Changed owners many times. William Jenkins gave him his freedom. Converted 1798. Became an Exhorter in 1835. Life-long member, Asbury MEC, Easton, MD. Died at age 103/4 years old

Noah Colwell W. Cannon – Born 1790. His father was a Methodist, and he grew up in Sussex County, Delaware. Raised in the Methodist Episcopal Church, he joined the AMEC when he moved to Philadelphia. He died in 1850 and was buried in Canada.

Benjamin Gibbs - Born 1798 in Kent County. Converted in 1815. In 1860 was ordained a Deacon. 1865 ordained Elder. Faithful member for 72 years.' Served Springtown Circuit.

Isaac Hinson - Born in 1799 in Kent County, Maryland, as a slave. At age 16, he purchased his freedom in New Jersey. By 1857 ordained an Elder. A Member of Colored Convention Meetings (Mt Zion Circuit). Served Zoar in 1859. For 16 years, used by the Presiding Elder by 1864

Simon Taylor - born (1799) in Port Penn, Delaware, as a slave. Became free at age 21. Converted in 1833. Licensed as Local Preacher: 1855 and Ordained Deacon: 1864.

Gabriel Friend - born (1800) and was ordained Deacon in 1850 in Preston-Bethesda Church. Ordained Elder 1865.

Angeline Taylor - born (1803 and married Rev. Simon Taylor.

William Frisby - born (1808) was licensed as an Exhorter in 1829 by Rev. Henry White, Presiding Elder. Licensed a Local Preacher in 1832. Ordained Deacon on July 30, 1865, by Bishop Levi Scott

John G. Manluff - born (1814) in Milford, Delaware. Converted in 1835. Was Licensed as an Exhorter, Local Preacher, and Ordained Deacon. By 1860 was an Ordained Elder. In 1859 was presented by Presiding Elder Urie (Wilmington District) was presented for an Appointment.

Charles Wing was born (1815 in Talbot County, Maryland. Licensed as an Exhorter in 1864 and Local Preacher in 1866.

Isaac Hemsley - born (1815 on the Eastern Shore of Maryland. Licensed as an Exhorter and Local Preacher

Joshua Brinkley - born (1816) in Wilmington, Delaware & did not know his parents. By 1857, Licensed Local Preacher. Ordained Deacon 1863. Ordained Elder July 28, 1864. 1857 served Odessa Circuit with Sam Dale

S. P. Marshall - born (1816) in Accomack County, Virginia. Converted very young. Mentioned in the 1867 Delaware Conference

Isaiah Broughton - born (1817 in Worcester County, Maryland, as a slave. Ordained Deacon by 1860. Owned by Judge Spence. Served Bay Shore Circuit, NJ 1858

Stephen Johns - born (1818) in Dorchester County, Maryland, into slavery and later was freed. Received on Trial at First Delaware Conference Session. Died August 17, 1879.

David Tilghman - born (1818) at Chestnut Hill, Pennsylvania. Converted 1842 in Boston. Was Licensed as a Local Preacher. Ordained Deacon 1848. Ordained Elder 1854

John C Carroll - born (1820) near Cambridge, Maryland. Converted in 1837. Licensed Local Preacher in 1867. Ordained Deacon in 1869. Free parents. He was known as 'Honest John'

Abraham Murray - born in Chestertown, Maryland. Rev. Joseph Lybrand, Presiding Elder, appointed him in 1840

Solomon Cooper - born (1824 in Easton, Maryland, as a slave. Converted in 1840 in Baltimore. 'He took the North Star. He returned after slavery ended.

Joseph D. Elbert - born (1827 in Kent County. Converted in 1837. Licensed Local Preacher in 1863. Ordained Deacon 1865

John H Holland - born (1828 in Anne Arundel County, Maryland. Converted early in his life. His mother was Sophie (free) & his father was Matthew (slave). In 1853, he moved to Federalsburg, Maryland

Hooper Jolly - born (1831). Converted in 1841. Licensed Exhorter in 1865. Licensed Local Preacher in 1866. Ordained Deacon 1867. Was Ordained Elder (nd). He served in the Newark Conference for 1 year.

Charles Ash - born (1832) in Caroline County, Maryland. Converted 1847. Licensed as Exhorter in 1866

Perry W. Pipes - born (1845). Converted early in his life. Ordained Deacon in 1876\

Jacob Gibson* - Born in slavery and later became free. Licensed Exhorter in 1835 by the Talbot Quarterly Conference. 1835-1836

went to Liberia and died shortly after arrival. His son, Joseph, becomes a government leader.

Stephen Wells - Licensed Exhorter in 1835 by the Talbot Quarterly Conference. Licensed Local Preacher in 1839 by Easton Quarterly Conference

Abraham Plater - Licensed Exhorter in 1835 by the Talbot Quarterly Conference, Maryland

Henry Cooper - Licensed Exhorter in 1835 by the Talbot Quarterly Conference, Maryland

Joseph Brice - Licensed Exhorter in 1835 by the Talbot Quarterly Conference, Maryland

Gildroy Henry - Licensed Exhorter in 1835 by the Talbot Quarterly Conference. Licensed Local Preacher in 1837 by Easton Quarterly Conference, Maryland

Aaron Wells - Licensed Exhorter 1835 by Talbot Quarterly Conference, Maryland

Charles Wells - Licensed Exhorter, 1835 by Talbot Quarterly Conference, Maryland

Cyrus Sinclair - Licensed Exhorter 1837

Joseph Brown - Licensed Exhorter 1840

Solomon Jackson – Born 1800. By 1840, he was licensed as a Local Preacher. By 1860, Ordained Deacon. Ordained Elder July 31, 1864, Married Civil War Soldiers. Lived in Cambridge.

Mary C Webb - born (1840) near Vienna, Maryland. Converted in 1855. Married Rev. J. E. Webb

Sarah E Johnson - born (1848) in Odessa, Delaware. Converted in 1860. Married Rev. T. H. Johnson

Elizabeth Winters - born (1832 in Queen Anne's County, Maryland. Married Rev. J. H. Winters

Samuel Green – born (1802?) East New Market (died February 28, 1877). Recommended by Sharp St & John Wesley Station for Appointment to Milford Circuit, Delaware in 1858.Imprisoned for having a copy of Uncle Tom's Cabin.

James Davis - born in Montgomery County, Maryland. Ordained Elder by 1857. Zoar Ch. Employed by Presiding Elder Coombe at Centreville in 1859

Samuel Dale -Born 1799. Ordained Elder in 1857. Ordained Elder by 1860. Served Odessa Circuit, Delaware

Harrison Smith – Born 1825. served in 1858 Springtown Circuit; Bay Shore Circuit. Died 1874.

Richard Crawford, by 1857, was a Licensed Local Preacher and associated with Zoar Church.

Peter Wise - by 1857 as ordained Deacon and associated with the John Wesley Church

Daniel Carter - associated with John Wesley Church

William Polk - by 1857 was a Licensed Local Preacher. Ordained Deacon in 1863. Lived in Milford, DE

Nathan Young – Born 1825 in Ellendale, DE By 1857, ordained Deacon. By 1860, ordained Elder. Founder of the Delaware Conference. Associated with Slaughter Neck, DE

Rendal Johnson - by 1857 Licensed Local Preacher. Associated with Springtown Circuit, NJ

Sherry E Adams - by 1857 Licensed Local Preacher. Associated with Williamsville

Rodger O. Adams - by 1857 Licensed Local Preacher. Associated with Williamsville. His death was recognized in 1859

William P. Gibson - by 1859, Licensed Local Preacher. Associated with Mt. Zion Circuit

Philip Scott - by 1857, ordained Elder. Associated with Ezion. In 1863, he would not take off his hat for soldiers. Associated with the Milford Circuit
John Fisher - by 1857 Licensed Local Preacher. Associated with Ezion

Alexander Lee - by 1857 ordained, a **Jacob Ivins** - by 1860 Licensed as Local Preacher Deacon, which means he was previously Licensed as a Local Preacher. Associated with Smyrna Circuit

Solomon Midcap - by 1857, Licensed as a Local Preacher. Associated with Slaughter Neck, DE

David Stevens - Associated with Zoar Church

Robert Davis - Associated with Zoar Church

Ebenezer Songs - by 1863 Licensed Local Preacher. 1857-Dover Circuit; 1858- Georgetown Circuit; 1859-Discontinued; 1863-Reinstated

Benjamin Brown - Associated Ezion-New Castle. Sec of Conf. 1859. 1860 Left for Baltimore

Silas Murray - by 1860 Licensed Local Preacher, Associated with Georgetown Cir./Smyrna/ Expelled 1863

Wilmore S. Elsey – born 1805 in Somerset County, MD. Served six years before 1864. Elected first Secretary of the Delaware Conference. Died August 5, 1867.

Jehu H. Pierce – Born 1827. By 1860, ordained a Deacon. Ordained Elder in 1863. He had been a Licensed Local Preacher earlier

Richard Moore – Born 1805. By 1863, Licensed as a Local Preacher. By 1860, ordained a Deacon. Gave Rev Samuel Green a copy of *Uncle Tom's Cabin,* who served time in jail for having that copy. Blacksmith. In the 1850 Census could not read or write.

William Gross - by 1860 Licensed as Local Preacher

Samuel Laws - by 1860, Licensed as a Local Preacher. Ordained Deacon in 1863

Robert Price - by 1860 Licensed as Local Preacher

Henry P. Gray - by 1860 Licensed as Local Preacher

Daniel R. Oney - by Abraham Brown - 1863 Licensed as Local Preacher. Associated with Cold Spring Circuit, then TBS 1860 Licensed as Local Preacher

Frost Pullet – Born 1788 in Princess Anne, Maryland. Member of the Manoken Quarterly Conference. First President of the Delaware Conference. Died 1872.

Samuel Spencer - in 1863, Licensed Local Preacher. Associated with Laurel Circuit

John W. Sander - by 1863 Licensed as Local Preacher

Emery Mines - by 1863 Licensed Local Preacher

Henry Liley - by 1863 Licensed Local Preacher

Solomon P. Young - by 1863 Licensed Local Preacher. Approved as Traveling Preacher

Peter Hill - by 1863 Licensed as Local Preacher

Henry Nelson - by 1863, ordained Deacon. He had earlier been licensed as a Local Preacher

Stephen Whittington - by 1863, ordained Deacon. He had earlier been licensed as a Local Preacher

Martin Spriddle - Maybe went to the Baltimore Conference

1838 – 1860 Exhorters Talbot County MD: Bingamon Johnson, Adam Wells, Thomas Hatheson (?), Richard Cooper, Greenburg Cooper, Walter Maxwell, Joseph Brown, Cyrus Sinclair, Benjamin Johnson, Samuel, Hamsley (?), Obediah Bentley, James Bantom, Standley Gardner, John Stevens, James Peck, Joseph Gibson, Daniel Miller, James Mitchell, Ishmail Johnson, Asbury Ridout, Joseph Johnson, Elbert Anderson, Abraham Frazier, Robert Warner, Charles Murray, Horace Lowery. (26) [56]

In 1832 Methodist Episcopal Church's General Conference supported a mission to Liberia under the auspices of the American Colonization Society, a movement to allow free blacks to return to Africa. It was modeled on the movement of Europeans to the American colonies. The places chosen were the islands and the coast of today's Liberia. The name means liberty. It was modeled on the personages of the American Revolution. It is noted here to illustrate the wide reach the Methodist Episcopal Church had in the lives of its African American members.

In Talbot County, **Jacob Gibson** took many of his family members in 1835 to Liberia. Although he died in March 1836, not long after he arrived, his son, Joseph, became a government leader whose name is known today in Liberia. *On Africa's Shore* gives a detailed treatment of the colonization movement.

African-American Methodist Membership: National & Mid-Eastern Shore, MD

QC=Quarterly Conference

Year	MEC	Phil Conf	Preacher	MEC, South	QC Dorchester	Preacher	QC Cambridge	Preacher	QC Church Creek	Preacher	TOTAL COUNTY Preacher	QC Talbot	QC Easton	TOTAL COUNTY
1788	6,545				264						264	524		524
1790	8,243				347						347	608		608
1795	12,170				406						406	266		266
1800	13,452				553						553	393		393
1805	24,316	8,914			827						827	849		849
1810	34,724	10,714			547		756				1303	916		916
1815	43,187	10,386			543		714				1,257	719		719
1820	38,753	8,279			622		606				1,228	600		600
1825	48,040	7,920			588		695				1,283	600		600
1830	69,383	8,169			611		721				1,332	637		637
1835	83,135	8,861			712		784				1,496	532		532
1840	102,158	8,778	38		672		805				1,477	447	159	606
1845	150,120	10,742		DIVISION	711		438		497		1,646	581	142	723
1850	26,309	8,406			680		407		300		1,387	328	312	640
1855	none	8,609	57		586	5	383	8	374	7	1,343	285	330	615
1860				171,857							20 Preachers			

Is Lewes, Delaware, the Oldest American Methodist Society?

Delaware is known as The First State because it was the first state to sign the U.S. Constitution. Should Delaware also be known as The First State to have an American Methodist Society?

E.C. Hallman's book, *Garden of Methodism*, is the source Lewes Methodists have used to date their beginnings. Hallman noted the Whitefield society was founded in 1739, but "for want of spiritual oversight and the opposition to it, it gradually died."[220] Hallamn dates the beginning of Methodism to the arrival of Freeborn Garrettson in 1779, the date currently used by Methodists to show how long they have been active in Lewes. Is Hallman correct?

To answer the question, first we first understand what is meant by 'being a Methodist.' Methodism stems from its formation at Oxford University as "The Holy Club." John Wesley was brought to the university to help improve the spiritual situation among the students. One student member was George Whitefield. Whitefield, along with the Wesley brothers, was ordained in the Anglican Church as a priest. When the Wesley brothers left for Georgia, Whitefield

---

220 E.C. Hallman, *Garden of Methodism* (Peninsula Annual Conference of the Methodist Church, 1947), page 262.

became the leader of this early group of Methodists. When they returned, Whitefield turned the leadership back to John Wesley, and he set off on his second of seven trips to America in 1739. The Methodist way was always preaching for people to have a 'new birth' experience and gather regularly in small groups to continue their spiritual development.

He put in place the Methodist practices Wesley had developed in England, as he traveled up and then down the east coast of the British American colonies. He was a commanding preacher. Large crowds of thousands gathered to hear him speak. Those who responded to his call for a new birth were gathered into weekly societies. His Methodist emphasis on the new birth experience over the Sacrament of Baptism put him at odds with the local clergy and divided Anglican church members who followed Whitefield's practice.

Lewes was the first stop when he disembarked in 1739 with his Methodist ways. His reputation in England followed him to Lewes. In response to his preaching, a Methodist society was born, about which the Rev. William Becket referred in his January 2, 1741, letter to Governor Thomas:

> Tho' my churches are full as ever Yet Mr Whitefield has dropt some of his Enthusiastic venom at Lewes I have not been there this fortnight the Weather is so bad. But they have set up a Society in my absence I ask'd the man that told me this what was the meaning of a Society. He told me they were to meet to sing Psalms & Hymns &c twice a week. There is no harm in the Affair, if there by no counter plot. But I cannot forbear suspecting that Whitefield & Tools have laid Schemes all over America, to draw people to dislike of our Church Doctrine Discipline & Government...[221]

---

[221] Nelson Waite Rightmyer, *The Anglican Church in Delaware*, p. 116)

Again, on April 25, 1741, Rev. Becket wrote to the Commissary Commings in Philadelphia:

> It is surprising to observe how the vulgar, everywhere are inclined to Enthusiasm. Mr Whitefield had a vast crowd of hearers at services in May last, where he preached 4 or 5 times from a balcony. I believe some times to … than 14 or 1,500 of all sorts. They had tried unknown to me to set up a Religious Society some of the church people (a few for they made up not above 30 of all sorts) joined them, but still they came to Church on Sunday. Holidays: by using them with Moderation prevails with those that us'd to receive the Sacrament not to break Church communion, so they rec'd on Easter Sunday. But this Humour of theirs seems like all other violent things not to be of long continuance, for they are dropping from one another both here and elsewhere thro' this Province, as I am informed. God only knows what may be the issue of these things at last. We can only trust in God & do our duty.[222]

There was no question from Hallman that a Methodist society was started. The question was about its continuation. From the Society for the Propagation of the Gospel Archives, eleven years after Rev Becket wrote to the Governor, the Methodist society was still meeting, because of Rev. Arthur Ussher's report to his SPG supervisor in London:

> …I have baptized 18 white children, 2 Negro children, and 1 adult white woman, after previous examination …my congregations daily increase, notwithstanding, efforts of the Methodists, to Disturb the peace of the Church. They seem rigid, but now, when they have not one of their own let (me) preach to them, they constantly come to Church, which makes me entertain some hope, that they will in God's due time unite with us at Lewes Church on Christmas Day…[223]

In the minds of the Anglican clergy, Whitefield and Methodists

---

222 SPG Archives, April 25, 1741. Transcribed by Gary L. Moore.
223 Ibid., 1751. Transcribed by Gary L. Moore.

were understood as a movement within the sphere of the Church of England. But the Methodists were disturbing what the Anglican clergy understood as congregational peace. This was the source of these clergy's anguish.

We are hindered in our understanding of Whitefield's American ministry because of the lack of research on how he funneled converts into small groups and other aspects of his ministry. As his ministry was reaching its peak, Whitefield died in 1770. Around that time, Wesley sent his lay preachers, Joseph Pilmore and Richard Boardman, to America in 1769.

Whitefield was a solo act and did not have associates to continue his ministry, whereas Wesley had his preachers. And a system of management. The missionaries Wesley sent to America saw themselves as starting Methodism anew, because they did not have a substantial connection to Whitefield. Wesley and Whitefield had grown apart for many years. When Wesley found preachers willing to travel to America, they were not in his inner circle, nor did he have much confidence in their usefulness to him. America was a sideshow for Wesley; England was the man event.

Between the time of Whitefield and the American-born Methodist circuit rider, Freeborn Garrettson, was the Revolutionary War. It had stopped the normal functioning of Methodist groups and most of American life. It is most likely the reason Lewes Methodists use today, the 1779 date, is that Garrettson restarted the original Whitefield Methodist society. According to Garrettson's diary, he is busy in that area of Delaware, establishing circuits and reconstituting existing societies (classes). He does not mention that he started new societies.

Garrettson had a lively interest in Whitefield from his mother, who had heard him preach before he was born. In his diary, he pays attention to those he met for whom Whitefield had had a profound effect on their lives. In 1778, eight years after Whitefield's death, a Dover merchant by the name of Pryor was "awakened" under Mr. Whitefield. In Quantico, Maryland, an old couple, the Riders, recalled: "Many years ago we heard Mr. Whitefield preach, and we were brought to taste the sweetness of religion."[224] The spiritual effects of Whitefield's ministry were noticed long after his death in the greater Lewes, Delaware area.

These are strong indications that Methodism took root in Lewes early in Whitefield's ministry. Rev. Becket noted the standard practices of Methodism: weekday society meeting to reinforce their spiritual lives and the sacramental ministry from the Anglican Church. Methodism did not die out in Lewes, as Hallman had thought, but was vital eleven years later in 1751. This is before both Strawbridge and Captain Webb came to America. Like the First State, Lewes could rightfully claim to be the first American Methodist society.

---

224 Nathan Bangs, *The Life of Freeborn Garrettson* (New York, J. Emory and B. Waugh, 1830), pages 76, 82-83, 96, 100.

BIBLIOGRAPHY/READING LIST

Primary Sources:

African Methodist Episcopal Hymnal (African Methodist Episcopal Church, 2000).

Asbury, Francis. *The Journal and Letters of Francis Asbury.* 3 vols. (Nashville: Abingdon Press, 1958)

Book of Discipline of the Methodist Episcopal Church. These have been printed every 4 years since 1784

Coker, Daniel. *"A Dialogue Between a Virginian and an African Minister."* (Baltimore: Benjamin Edes, 1810).

Coker, Daniel. *Journal of Daniel Coker: A Descendant of Africa, From the time of leaving New York in the Ship Elizabeth, Capt. Seber, on a Voyage for Sherbro, in Africa* (Published by Edward J. Coale, 1820).

Cox, Lewis Y. *Pioneer Footprints* (Cape May, NJ: Star and Wave Press, 1917).

Easton Gazette, Vol. LVI, Issue 28, page 3 (Saturday, July 19, 1873).

Easton Quarterly Conference Minutes: 1835-1865. Unpublished.

General Minutes of the Methodist Episcopal Church. 1784-1939

General Minutes of the Methodist Episcopal Church, South. 1845-1939

Hall, Richard. *On Afric's Shore: A History of Maryland in Liberia, 1834-1857,* (The Maryland Center for History and Culture, 2004).

Journals of the Delaware Annual Conference. 1864-1965

Journals of the Philadelphia Annual Conference. 1843-1939.

Long, John D. *Pictures of Slavery in Church and State.* (Philadelphia, 1857).

Lee, Jarena, *Religious Experience and Journal of Mrs. Jarena Lee.* (Philadelphia, 1849).

Lee, Jesse. *A Short History of the Methodists.* (Baltimore: Magill & Clime, 1810).

Minutes of the General Conference of Methodist Episcopal Church. 1784-1939

Proceedings of the Ecumenical Methodist Conference, held in City Road Chapel, London, September 1881: Cincinnati (Walden and Stowe, 1882).

Ridgway, James, *Diary* (transcribed by Emma Ditman). Unpublished.

Society of Propagation of Gospel microfilm records, British Online Archives.

Talbot County Court Records, Easton, Maryland. From 1661.

Talbot Quarterly Conference Minutes: 1805-1865. Unpublished.

Wayman, Alexander W., *Cyclopedia of African Methodism* (Baltimore: Methodist Episcopal Book Depository), 1882.

Works of John Wesley (Nashville: Abingdon Press, 1984)

Whitefield, George, *George Whitefield's Journals* (Lafayette: Sovereign Grace, 2000).

Secondary Sources:

Andrews, Dee E., *The Methodists and Revolutionary America, 1760-1800.* (Princeton University Press, 2000).

Baker, Frank, *From Wesley to Asbury.* (Durham: Duke University Press, 1976).

Baldwin, Lewis, *Invisible Strands of African Methodism: A History of the African Union Protestant and Union American Methodist Episcopal Churches* (1805-1980). (ATLA monograph series, Scarecrow Press, 1984)

Bangs, Nathan, *The Life of Freeborn Garrettson,* (New York, J. Emory and B. Waugh, 1830).

Bangs, Nathan, *A History of the Methodist Episcopal Church,* four volumes (New York: G. Land & C.B. Tippett, 1845).

Bantu, Vince L. *A Multitude of All Peoples* (Downers Grove: InterVarsity Press, 2020).

Barclay, Wade Crawford, *History of Methodist Missions:1769-1844* (Board of Missions and Church Extension of The Methodist Church, 1949).

Bonomi, Patricia U., *Under the Cope of Heaven* (Oxford Press, 1986, 2003).

Bradley, David Henry Sr, *A History of the A.M.E. Zion Church Part 1* (Nashville: United Methodist Publishing, 1956).

Dallimore, Arnold, *George Whitefield* 2 vols. (London: Banner of Truth Trust, 1970).

Dorsey, Jennifer Hull, *Hirelings: African American Workers and Free Labor in Early Maryland* (Cornell University Press, 2011).

Elder, Robert, *Calhoun: American Heretic* (New York: Basic Books, 2021). Gray, Richard, *Black Christians & White Missionaries* (New Haven: Yale University Press, 1990).

Gray, Richard, and ed. Lamin Sanneh, *Christianity, The Papacy, and Mission in Africa* (Maryknoll: Orbis Books, 2012).

Hallman, E.C. *The Garden of Methodism* (Peninsula Annual Conference of the Methodist Church, n.d.)

Hatch, Nathan. *The Democratization of American Christianity* (New Haven: Yale University, 1989).

Handy, James A., *Scraps of African Methodist Episcopal History* (Philadelphia: A.M.E. Book Concern, 1902).

Kidd, Thomas S. *George Whitefield: America's Spiritual Founding Father* (New Haven: Yale University Press, 2014).

Lakey, Othal Hawthorne, *The History of the CME Church* (The CME Publishing House, 1985).

Larson, Kate Clifford, *Bound for the Promised Land: Harriet Tubman: Portrait of an American Hero* (One World. Ballantine Books, 2004).

McTyeire, Holland Nimmons, *A History of Methodism,* Nashville: Publishing House of MEC, South, 1884).

Melton, J. Gordon, *A Will to Choose: The Origins of African American Methodism* (Rowman & Littlefield Publishers, 2007).

Newman, Richard S. *Freedom's Prophet: Bishop Richard Allen, the AME Church, and the Black Founding Fathers* (New York University Press, 2008).

Norwood, Frederick A., *The Story of American Methodism* (Abingdon Press, 1974).

Oden, Thomas C., *The African Memory of Mark* (Downers Grove: Inter-Varsity Press, 2011).

Rack, Henry D. *Reasonable Enthusiast: John Wesley and the Rise of Methodism* (Philadelphia: Trinity Press, 1989).

Richey, Russell E., *The Methodist Conference in America: A History* (Abingdon Press, 1996).

Thomas, James S. *Methodism's Racial Dilemma: The Story of the Central Jurisdiction* (Nashville: Abingdon Press, 1992).

Walls, William J., *The African Methodist Episcopal Zion Church: Reality of the Black Church* (A.M.E. Zion Publishing House, 1974).

Wigger, John, *American Saint: Francis Asbury and The Methodists* (Oxford Press, 2009).

Wilford, John Noble. "Ezekiel's Wheel Ties African Spiritual Traditions to Christianity." *New York Times*, November 7, 2016. Used by permission (License Agreement # REF 000123773)

Williams, William H., *The Garden of American Methodism: The Delmarva Peninsula 1769—1820*, (Commission on Archives and History of the Peninsula—Delaware Conference of The United Methodist Church, 1984, 2009)

Research Centers:

Barratt's Chapel Museum and Archives, 6362 Bay Road, PO Box 668, Frederica, DE 19946. www.barrattschapel.org

Edward H. Nabb Research Center for Delmarva History and Culture, Guerrieri Academic Commons, 4th Floor, Room 430, Salisbury University, Salisbury, MD. nabbcenter@salisbury.edu

General Commission on Archives and History, Drew University, 36 Madison Avenue, PO Box 127, Madison, NJ 07940. www.gcah.org

United Methodist Historical Society of the Baltimore-Washington Conference, 2200 St. Paul Street, Baltimore, MD 21218. archives—history@bwcumc.org.

INDEX

ABOUT THE AUTHOR

Rev. Moore is a United Methodist ordained clergy, who has lived on the Delmarva Peninsula for over fifty years and served as President of the Peninsula-Delaware Conference's Commission on Archives and History. In this position he chaired the Delaware (Black) Conference History Commemorative booklet and conducted oral histories of Delaware Conference leaders.

Besides his interest in history, he served as a Chaplain in the Delaware National Guard for twenty-five years and is a graduate from the Command and General Staff Course. Following the 9/11 attack, he was deployed to the Pentagon, as the liaison between the National Guard Bureau and the Army Chief of Chaplains Offices for family support. He is married to Jeanne and they have five adult children. He resides in Easton, Maryland, the colonial capital of the Eastern Shore.